DEEP BLACK AND DANGEROUS

David Griffin

... I feel it right to warn the house that hostile intrigue and espionage are being relentlessly maintained on a large scale.

The Prime Minister, 14th November 1962

... Despite the Cold War ending nearly two decades ago, my service is still expending resources to defend the UK against attempts by Russia, China and others to spy on us.

Director General of the Security Service, 7th October 2007

Pen Press

© David Griffin 2008

All rights reserved

No part of this publication may be reproduced,
stored in a retrieval system, or transmitted
in any form or by any means, without
the prior permission in writing of the publisher,
nor be otherwise circulated in any form of binding or cover other than
that in which it is published and without a similar condition including
this condition being imposed on the subsequent purchaser.

First published in Great Britain by
Indepenpress Publishing Ltd
25 Eastern Place
Brighton BN2 1GJ

ISBN 978-1-906710-15-6

Hermes Publications
PO Box 3237
Bournemouth BH2 5YP

Printed and bound in the UK
by Cpod Trowbridge, Wiltshire

A catalogue record of this book is available from
the British Library

Cover design by noahsart: www.noahsart.co.uk
and dupli-k8 email dupli-k8@ukf.net

Acknowledgements

The Central Office of Information

Most of the briefings in this book were produced by COI's reference arm for distribution among civil servants circa last Cold War period. All the original records relating to it have now been destroyed.

The original booklet was called *Their Trade Was Treachery*, which I have now rewritten/updated and designed as a publication of information, education and awareness to an increasingly remote public.

I use the word 'remote' for good reason.

As recently as forty years ago there were very few families in Britain who could not talk of, in fine detail, their home county regiments, their local police forces, and most aspects of vigilance, duty and responsibility.

I personally fear that the closure of National Service went a long way in tearing and unravelling what was a tightly knitted Britain, to the 'remote' country that we see today, where every catastrophe has to have a 'scapegoat'.

Unfortunately, the ones who seldom escape unscathed are the Intelligence Services, the Soldier or the Police Officer.

From the above organisations there are sometimes totally unreasonable, and often impossible expectations.

I hope the bleak and cold hard facts of this book will educate the sceptics and put the record straight.

The material from *Their Trade Was Treachery* and all the photographs were, are, and will remain Crown Copyright, courtesy of COI.

David Griffin
January 2008

Illustrations

Some people who helped the Communists   24

Tools of the Spy   42

Contents

Foreword	1
How The Spy Machine Was Built	4
The Approach At Home	11
The Approach From Abroad	32
How Do We Stand?	49
How To Avoid Acts Of Treason	54
How To Engage In Treason	55
Security Defences	56
How To Foil A Spy	57
Conclusive Brief	60
The State of Play	65

This book is dedicated to
Tom & Des
"Warriors of Old Albion"

As is the following poem found in an envelope left by a soldier killed by an explosion near Londonderry in 1989.

It was read aloud by his father on the BBC television programme Bookworm, on Rememberance Sunday 1995.

And to the lives and times of all those service personnel who have made that ultimate sacrifice...

> *Do not stand at my grave and weep,*
> *I am not there, I do not sleep.*
> *I am the thousand winds that blow,*
> *I am the diamond glints on snow,*
> *I am the sunlight on ripened grain,*
> *I am the gentle autumn rain.*
> *When you awaken in the morning's hush,*
> *I am the swift uplifting rush,*
> *Of quiet birds in circled flight.*
> *I am the soft stars that shine at night.*
> *Do not stand at my grave and cry,*
> *I am not there;*
> *I did not die*
>
> *- Unknown*

Repro by David Griffin for Deep Black & Dangerous

Three things in particular are needed to protect our secrets from hostile Intelligence Services.

They are: INTEGRITY
            COMMON SENSE
            KNOWLEDGE

These will aid the defences of our way of life.

These will prevent national and personal tragedies.

It is when one or other is absent that the hostile Intelligence Service gets through to its intended target.

This book cannot enforce INTEGRITY and COMMON SENSE. It can only point out the consequences of a lack of them. I have tried to provide some basic knowledge.

David Griffin

Foreword

THE SPY GAME

It is often said and probably true, two of the oldest professions in the world are prostitution and spying. If the former is a reasonable assumption then the later is certainly true. More so because it involves the survival of the Tribe.

From those long gone days when we abandoned walking like apes and stood up on two feet, the Neanderthal soon learned the art and stealth of sneaking around a hillside to see what the opposition were up to down in yonder valley, as it were.

That was spying!

When the stalking fox will only approach the henhouse when the farmhouse lights have dimmed for the night and the coast is clear.

That is spying!

When McLaren Formula 1 motors steal blueprints from the offices of Ferrari, (allegedly).

That is spying!

And why! Because forearmed, as mentioned ensured the survival of the Tribe.

Those who choose to partake in the Spy Game must from the very outset learn to distinguish fact from fiction. Spying can be twenty-four hours per day a nerve-racking, dark, grubby and deceitful existence for the field operative.

To qualify this let me assure you of some facts of the profession.

For most operatives today, just like our old friend "Neanderthal Spy", make no mistake, there are no multifunctional "Omega" watches, there are no Bentley B-type Continentals hidden in the forest, there are no silky-smooth dinner jackets reeking of Paco Rabanne, and there are certainly no international ladies-of-the-night lurking or slithering around the casinos of Monte Carlo awaiting the attention of MI6 agents!

The reality is somewhat different. Ian Fleming and Sebastian Faulks have given us best selling fiction novels and films but in this book, in short non-fiction and to compliment all the great spy stories since the last cold war, I want to bring you back down to earth and reality.

There are very few people in the world today who can resist the excitement and lift, the glamour and fantasy of a good James Bond caper.

The life and style, the gadgets, equipment and power makes a simple man 'king for a day'.

But of the tens of millions of avid fans around the world today, I would wager there are pitiful few who know or understand the deep black and dangerous existence of the real-life covert operative. Those who are willing, on behalf of their country, to infiltrate the enemy theatre to steal their secrets.

Equally dangerous are those in positions of trust who choose to betray their country and sell secrets to an enemy. To those who think this way, I would warn there is a line which must not be crossed.

If they choose to step on that line they should be mindful.

"Beyond this place there are dragons."

In the following briefs I will explain how the "Bear Trap" of treason is open to all from office clerk to CEO, from private soldier to top politician or cabinet minister. For those foolish enough to cross the line, that glittering neon sign above the "Bear Trap" is forever blinking, "We never close, come and talk to us". DON'T!

During the latter part of 2006 a military aid to General David Richards, the then Commander of the British forces in Afghanistan appeared in court accused of spying. Corporal Daniel James was charged under the 1911 Official Secrets Act with "prejudicing the safety of the State" by passing information "calculated to be directly or indirectly useful to the enemy." This enemy was believed to be Iran.

Daniel James was 44 and a T.A. soldier from Brighton and being Iranian born, he was used as an interpreter on the General's staff.

Cpl. James will attend the Old Bailey in 2008 for trial (subject to evidence).

Cpl. James had crossed the line and met the dragons.

Spies are with us all the time.

They are interested in everything, defence secrets, scientific secrets, political decisions, economic facts; even people's characters – in order to recruit more spies.

In this book I will tell you how to recognise at once certain espionage techniques and how to avoid crossing the line into "Dragonland", which could lead to a national catastrophe or, as in the case of Cpl. James, a very personal disaster, or both.

They may be closer than you think!

How The Spy Machine Was Built

"MOTHER RUSSIA"

During the first cold war, before we watch the machine working at close hand, let us see how it was constructed. Some understanding of this may give us clues as to how to oppose it.

The basic fact we had to face was that the Intelligence Service of the Soviet Union, combined with those of Russia's communist governed allies, was the biggest machine for the garnering of secret information which the world had ever known.

The Russian, the Eastern European and the Balkan peoples under their domination, through centuries of conspiracy against autocratic regimes, had learned to combine an aptitude for intrigue with an acquired guile – as had other nations similarly placed.

Necessity, born of bitter experience – sometimes, fatal experience – had taught them to be secretive and secure, patient and unhurried.

Furthermore, for reasons of internal security, as well as external spying, the old Soviet Intelligence Service had always been regarded by the Russian Government with the same esteem as other countries would accord to their armies, navies, and air forces, and had received a commensurate amount of material and moral support.

It was therefore not only large and backed with ample resources; it was able to mix, and to a dangerous degree, what we might call inborn talent with then modern experience and methods.

It was a big machine. It was efficient.

If we appeared first to concentrate our attention upon the Soviet part of the spy machine rather than upon those of its allies, this was simply because the Soviet Intelligence Service was the main dynamo of the formidable apparatus which was in constant motion against us.

This did not mean that the other parts of the overall spy machine were to be ignored, as you will read later in these pages; although each of the Iron Curtain countries ran their own intelligence gathering service, the Soviet one, as the oldest and most powerful, had lent them aid and training knowledge, and indeed, to a certain extent, continued to direct them, overtly or otherwise.

Fortunately, although their combined efforts were of menacing proportions, the situation was not hopeless, because like all monster organisations this one had its weak points.

It could be combated by common sense, good will, and a wider knowledge of how this big beast functioned.

Let us now look closer.

Again, during the first cold war there were two main branches of the Russian Intelligence Service:

1. The GRU
   This directed military, naval and air espionage in all foreign countries.

2. The KGB
   This attended to all the other intelligence needs of the Soviet Government.

The Intelligence Services of Russia's (then) European communist allies were organised into somewhat similar branches and in some measure operated on similar lines.

'Legal' and 'Illegal' Spying

Russian spy networks were of two types. One was the kind which the Russians were pleased to call the 'Legal' apparatus.

(Although many of my referrals are of a past tense cold war, I think it is true to say many of the old methods still work well today.)

The 'Legal' network was under the control of a member of the Soviet Embassy staff who was referred to in Russian espionage jargon as 'The Resident'. He enjoyed diplomatic immunity. There was, of course, little that was legal about his activities.

So, although any British subjects who happened to work for him at the embassy were liable to imprisonment, the worst that could happen to 'The Resident', he would be declared **Persona non grata** – at least until he was called upon, in Moscow, to explain his mistakes.

The Russians called the other spy network, which would have no connection with the Soviet Embassy, the 'Illegal' apparatus.

A classic example of an 'Illegal' resident was the spy master who called himself Lonsdale, who directed a network of British traitors, and who was, in fact, a Russian officer posing as a businessman.

The 'Illegal' resident would have no connection with any official Russian organisation in the country in which he operated, and no diplomatic immunity. He could be sent to prison, as Lonsdale was.

So, the above is just a mild explanation of the 'Legal' and 'Illegal' operators who are, and have always been in our midst.

Talent Spotting

Before they can obtain the secret information they seek, the enemy Intelligence Services must first find people who can get it or may be able to get it in the future, and then they must gather personality reports about such people to access their vulnerability to persuasion or pressure. This grooming process is known as **Talent Spotting.**

From time immemorial and certainly today, their victims, willing or otherwise, fell into three categories:

> **The Ideological Spy** – who thinks the enemy's cause is more just than his own country's, or has other reasons which he thinks good and ethical.
>
> **The Mercenary Spy** – who works for money only.
>
> **The Spy Under Pressure** – who has been compromised either in Britain or Russia, or is an émigré with relatives in enemy block territory.

Of all spies, the ideological one is perhaps the hardest to uncover – especially if his conversion to the enemy cause has taken place after he has been given a position of trust. We can see this age-old method at work today in the 2008 case at the Old Bailey of Cpl. Daniel James accused of spying for Iran while on the staff of General David Richards, in Afghanistan.

This type of spy may not even be paid for his treachery and thus perhaps draw attention to himself by spending more than his apparent income – and he may have taken the precaution of keeping his conversion quiet.

Such a man was George Blake of the Foreign Office. We will come to him later.

So, if we break down these three categories we will then be able to list the wide range of weapons that are at the disposal of a spy master in his search for recruits.

The Ideological Spy

The ideological spy may work for the overthrow of this county's institutions because he believes that communism or his own favoured regime is the best political system for Britain and that only by the downfall of the present ruling class can it be achieved. He is not democratically interested in the fact that the majority of the people may not want such a programme. He knows what is best and what the country needs. Or so he thinks.

The ideological spy may believe that the Western World is plotting war, and think, in some twisted way that by helping our potential enemies, he will make them so strong that the Western World will be afraid to attack them, or that by supplying them with secret political information he will enable Russia or others to forestall the so-called war plans of Britain and America and thus preserve peace. This is particularly so in this new twenty-first century where Russia bangs on a new set of war drums and the "third world", as we have the audacity to call it, is now armed to the teeth and ripe for chaos on a global scale.

The ideological spy may claim that all scientific knowledge, even that involving his country's most vital secrets, should be shared with other countries no matter what the regime.

Of such a type was the atom spy Alan Nunn May, who, with the other scientific spy, Dr Klaus Fuchs, received little of no money for his deadly work.

There are indeed no limits to the labyrinth in arguments which an ideological spy may employ to justify his actions. His principal characteristic is intellectual arrogance.

The Mercenary Spy

The mercenary spy is motivated by greed or possibly what, at the beginning of his spy career, he might sometimes tell himself is necessity.

Vassall, the Admiralty spy, claimed that at first he was blackmailed, but later he clearly became a mercenary spy.

Unlike his ideological comrade in treachery, who often received little or no money, the mercenary spy may call attention to himself because he is a person, known to be entrusted, with secrets, and because he lives at a standard above his ostensible income.

Ex-Petty Officer Houghton, in the Portland Naval case, was primarily a mercenary spy. He overspent and the fact was noted.

The Spy Under Pressure

The spy under pressure is a person who has been blackmailed. With one possible exception, noted below, he is a person of weak moral fibre, who sinks deeper into the mire because he lacks the courage to face up to the consequences of some past crime or even some mere indiscretion. Rather than do so, he prefers to face far graver consequences in the future.

He may be a man confronted with an accusation of a homosexual act, either true or faked by a hostile intelligence service. He may be trying to live down some past dishonesty or to hide almost anything which he fears of being exposed.

The **émigré** is perhaps the one exception mentioned above. He may have to make a terrible choice: to betray the country of his adoption or to expose loved members of his family, still living under communist rule or that of a hostile regime, to terrible threat and consequences.

Whatever his choice, it might be argued that it could call for a tragic decision which would not necessarily be rooted in a lack of moral courage.

Whichever way he chooses, and however great his former integrity, if he is a man of honour and sensitivity, his tranquillity of mind is doomed.

The Armoury

We now see the main armoury at the disposal of the spy master: ideals – however twisted.

1. Money and all it will buy.
2. Fear and all its by-products.
3. But there is a secondary armoury which must not be forgotten.
   And we may be sure that the spy master knows how to draw upon it.

   Sexual attraction.

   Conceit and vanity.

   Sense of power – of being part of a strong machine.

   Love of intrigue.

   Feeling of importance.

   Desires for praise and flattery, and that very old chestnut – a chip on the shoulder.

The weapons are many. The selection of which to use depends upon the assessment of the victim's character, and the observations of the spy master himself.

The Social Approach

When the spy master, whether by chance or by cautious machinations, makes personal contact with a potential agent, he often employs a standard technique, which in counter-espionage language is called the social approach.

The pattern of social approaches made covering both sexes, all grades of society, and many different occupations, especially approaches to the military, reveals four interesting aspects:

1. The apparently innocent manner in which the first personal contact, if a planned one, is made by the spy master, whether he is 'Legal' or 'Illegal'; for however much preliminary work may have been done by lesser fry such as talent spotters, this personal contact must be made in the end.

2. The equally innocent manner in which a 'friendship' is then fostered, without the potential recruit suspecting ulterior motives.
3. The incredible patience employed. Cases are known in which the ostensible 'friendship' has been developed over many years without any further progress being seemingly made. But during this time we can be sure that the dossier will have grown thicker as the spy master painstakingly notes his quarry's faults, virtues, changing circumstances, the details of their various meeting places and what was discussed and done, together with copies of the messages which would be sent to Moscow or another hostile regime, and the instructions received from the spy centres of those regimes.
4. The extraordinary detailed control often exercised by the control centre over every activity of its spy master abroad. Although the old Iron Curtain Secret Services had their centres, this was especially true of their Soviet centre, which had been known to give instructions about the exact place, time, and circumstances when some meetings were to take place in far away London.

These instructions were always carried out to the letter.

The hostile talent spotters ranged widely. Here are some of the fields in which they were known to have been at work in Australia in the first cold war:

> The Department of External Affairs
> Foreign diplomatic missions
> Members of Parliament
> Journalists
> Commercial aides
> Scientists
> Counter-espionage and security organisations
> **Émigrés** circles

These facts, and many others, are now known because a Russian Intelligence Officer, called Petrov, defected in Australia, and a report was subsequently produced by the Australian authorities. The report had a chapter ominously entitled "Operations Towards Setting an Illegal Apparatus in Australia."

The Approach At Home

Before we come to the more repellent activities of hostile intelligence services when operating against British and other nationalities serving in communist or other dictatorial nations, let us just watch exactly how they have in the past, and still do use the social friendly approach in Britain.

Here are some typical cases:

A Mouse Called Lloyd

This story begins pleasantly enough at a trade reception and ends drearily in an Assize Court (in Britain pre-1971).

Given the weak character of the central figure, and the strains and stresses to which he was suddenly submitted, it seems with hindsight that it was almost inevitable that it should have a bad ending.

Yet had he read the signals correctly, Lloyd might have been saved.

He didn't, and he was lost. Here is what happened.

The Watchful Colonel

To Colonel Novak, the Military Attaché, the reception was little different from many others he had attended. It was just one of those occasions when commercial firms were there to meet potential foreign customers. A routine affair. Drink flows. Everybody is friendly. Valuable personal trade contacts can be made, and often are made.

Colonel Novak, outwardly pleasant and relaxed, prowled among the guests, exchanging a handshake here, a few words there. He too was seeking valuable personal contacts.

But they were not trade contacts. Alert and experienced, he began to try to separate the potentially useful people from the obviously useless ones. We do not know what other contacts he may have made, but we do know that suddenly, at that reception fraught with much consequence for Britain, Colonel Novak found himself talking to a man called Lloyd.

Colonel Novak saw to it that the talk was a long and cordial one. He had every reason to do so, after he had learned that Lloyd was an electronics engineer.

When they finally parted and went their separate ways, the electronics engineer called Lloyd had the friendly Colonel's address in his pocket.

More important, the friendly Colonel had Lloyd's address.

If Lloyd forgot about Colonel Novak in the ensuing weeks, the Colonel did not forget about Lloyd. In Novak's profession one does not forget about meetings with electronics engineers, even ordinary fellows like Lloyd, and, as Novak was to discover, Lloyd was certainly ordinary. He didn't drink or bet much, or have mistresses, or have homosexual tendencies. In fact, he lived quite a normal life, with a wife, a good job, and every prospect of a happy and honourable retirement.

He was indeed so ordinary that even when the telephone rang one day, and he heard the voice of Colonel Novak inviting him and his wife to an embassy reception, he politely declined.

Perhaps he felt that ordinary people like him and his wife would be socially at a disadvantage in diplomatic circles. Perhaps some inner monitoring voice warned him that acceptance might spell danger.

Was this a come-on?

Was the Colonel talent spotting?

Whatever his feeling this is the point at which he should have gone straight to the top of his employment tree for fine-tuning on security matters. Later indeed, when he was being interrogated, he claimed, with a pathetic attempt at pompous dignity, that he refused because he was "not at all sure of the gentleman's status in this country." Better for Lloyd if his inner voice had spoken up louder in the years ahead.

Better for Britain, too.

The Hospitable Colonel

Colonel Novak was rebuffed but not defeated. He was a patient man. He was trained to be. Mulling over the notes he had made about his talk with Lloyd, he realised he had been too crude. The social approach covers a multitude of sins and though Lloyd had no apparent sins to exploit, Colonel Novak's notes yielded one important fact.

Lloyd loved music.

Music had been enthusiastically discussed, by them both, at the trade reception. Music might draw them together again, might form the cement in a long and profitable friendship.

Putting it another way, music might represent the cheese to entice the mouse if not into the trap at least towards it.

More hopeful now, believing that he had found the right bait, perhaps blaming himself for not thinking of it before, the hospitable Colonel Novak invited Lloyd and his wife to a concert at the Royal Festival Hall, and to supper afterwards.

The offer proved irresistible. Lloyd accepted. Poor foolish mouse.

The Patient Colonel

We have mentioned that time means little or nothing to the Russians or other hostile nations. It meant nothing back in the first cold war nor does it in the emerging new cold war of this twenty-first century, so it is interesting to see what happened next.

For two long years the grey men at Colonel Novak's particular centre sat back and watched while the friendship matured between Novak and his wife and Lloyd and Mrs Lloyd.

They saw how the Lloyds and the Novaks were soon visiting each other's homes, and how the Novaks even attended the reception at the wedding of the Lloyd's oldest daughter and they were content with the Colonel's progress and grooming. It often went this way. It's happening here in Britain today.

The temptation to act prematurely, to try to learn and glean from Lloyd the secrets he must be able to obtain, would at times have been overpowering. But they did not press. They maintained the patience and covert invisibility of the lion in pampas grass. And Novak himself did not put a foot wrong.

All was sweetness and light and music, and a professed desire by the Novaks to compare normal English life with Russian life – as good an excuse as any for a diplomat to put forward when mixing with an electronics engineer in a different station in life.

It might not deceive many people. It should not deceive anybody. It deceived Lloyd.

Meanwhile there was orchestrated normality. The centre waited. Novak waited. The time was not ripe. But at least the mouse had become used to the cage-trap and was enjoying the cheese. Somewhere, some place, sometime, an opportunity would arise to drop the door. But when?

The chance came in 1957.

At the end of 1956 Lloyd had joined another electronics firm on the south coast.

The following March his family joined him at the house he had taken in Worthing. It was a disastrous move for all concerned. Domestic trouble arose, swelled and reached explosion point, and Mrs Lloyd, no longer able to tolerate the position, left her husband.

Lloyd, worried by debts (increased by the acquisition of a mistress), suffering from terrible strain, encumbered by an aged and senile mother whose continued presence in his house had at least partly caused his domestic troubles, now faced the future – to all intents and purposes alone.

When Colonel Novak heard of these delightful matters, he knew his time had come. The long days and months of waiting were over. Check the trap door. It was now or never.

The Benevolent Colonel

In the one hand, tea, sympathy and friendship. In the other, hard cash to pay his debts. These were the gifts Colonel Novak offered to the mouse called Lloyd when they dined, ever so discreetly, in a Soho restaurant a little later.

If Lloyd felt a twinge of alarm at the mention of money, if he suddenly wondered whether, after all, Novak was entirely disinterested – and there is no evidence that he did – the Colonel soon put his mind at ease.

All he wanted were a few catalogues and brochures about electronics in general. That's all. Harmless enough, surely? Almost the sort of thing one friend would do for another without any payment at all.

So, when Colonel Novak suggested they should meet in Brighton in June, Lloyd was willing enough. He had only to come along the coast from Worthing, and a breath of sea air would doubtless be welcome to the Colonel. He agreed to meet Novak near one of the piers.

Foolish Lloyd. Stupid mouse.

But when Lloyd had handed over his catalogues and brochures at Brighton in June, and when he had opened the envelope Novak gave him, and saw the £50 in it, he must have thought that some friendships pay off better than others.

At this point in our story it is worth remembering as we speak now in this twenty-first century, that £50 back in the fifties was a very lucrative pay packet for one day in Brighton.

Perhaps he thought Novak's next meeting place, a crossroad near Worthing, a little odd, even if convenient. If he did, he crushed the thought. He agreed to the meeting.

Looking back (and remember this is going on in many Western countries even today), it was plain to see the cage door was closing fast.

It closed completely after the meeting at the crossroads.

Novak said the catalogues were not quite what he wanted. Then came the mother of all punch lines: He stressed his interest in Radar.

Significantly, he omitted doing one thing, which he had done at the previous meeting. He handed over no money.

Significantly, too, he again suggested a road junction for the next meeting.

Now was literally the moment of truth.

Even the very foolish Lloyd could no longer persuade himself that the benevolent Colonel Novak was prepared to trade good money, and lots of it, for mere catalogues.

Now was the last chance to draw back from this edge of the espionage trap. Others had done it before him, and others would do so after him. Not so Lloyd. He agreed to the meeting, and all that that implied.

With his eyes wide open to what he was doing, he crossed the threshold of the cage for the last time, and the trapdoor crashed down behind him. Henceforth he was the prisoner of a hostile intelligence service. A willing prisoner. Ironically they never had to blackmail him.

The social approach had lured him: a taste for money had trapped him; he was now a traitor selling his country's secrets for cash. It had become as simple as that.

The money was useful and he could always do with more of it.

From this time onwards his descent was rapid.

Although what I brief you on now were events happening from 1945 through to the late 1960s make no mistake about it, these tried and tested patterns have never lost ground, so whoever came up with that old adage – "If it ain't broken, don't fix it" certainly had it right. Hostile intelligence agencies are well aware of this and it's happening today in Britain and all over the West. Be advised of this.

Our treacherous friend had every right to go to a cupboard where secret blueprints were kept. So meetings were planned for weekends, because at Lloyd's place of employment some of the staff worked on Saturday mornings.

On Saturday mornings, Lloyd extracted material.

On Saturday afternoons, he gave it to Colonel Novak.

On Sundays Novak gave it back, having photocopied it.

Secret ways were evolved to inform Lloyd of the place, date, and time of meetings and now Novak showed an interest in things other than radar.

To Lloyd the payments seemed good.

> In October 1957 Lloyd received £50
>
> In December, it was £100
>
> In January 1958 it was £50
>
> In February, it was £200

Let me remind you again of the value of such figures at that time.

End of the Road

But now events took a curious shape. At the February meeting, the documents were not returned by Novak, but by a deputy, who said that Novak was sick.

A further meeting with Novak was nevertheless arranged for 29th March 1958.

Lloyd waited in vain.

Colonel Novak did not arrive. Colonel Novak's deputy did not arrive. Perhaps the Colonel sensed he was under suspicion.

Perhaps the unusually large sum of £200 was a farewell gift of cash to a man who would certainly need it in the future. Not that there was much future left now.

Lloyd was never met again by his spy master or even his deputy.

Instead, in May 1958, at a time and place of their own choosing he was met by a different set of people, arrested, put on trial at the Assize Court (a special court in Britain until 1971) and sentenced to fourteen years imprisonment and in those halcyon days of justice it meant all of fourteen years.

Poor, silly, treacherous Lloyd.

After his sentence, he thought he had been harshly treated. Some idea of his twisted thinking can be seen from the following incident.

At one stage, Novak proposed a "Dead letter box", a hiding place where the documents could be concealed, collected by Novak, and a little later recovered by Lloyd. Lloyd refused to cooperate. He said he thought it was "underhanded".

The Reasons Why

He fell because he did not recognise the social approach when it happened; because he did not honestly ask himself whether it was likely that a diplomat like Colonel Novak would need to mix with Lloyd's family to learn of English ways: because in his straits he could not resist money; and because Novak played gently with him, at first whetting his appetite for money by paying a lump sum in exchange for innocuous catalogues.

And it all began with a trade reception – and a talk about music.

The name of the man was Lloyd, but it might have been Brown, or Smith or Jones, or any man or woman who does not understand the social approach or appreciate that big diplomatic cats do not normally play with humble mice without good reason and a hope of profit.

Who's for Tennis?

Sometimes hostile intelligence services employ unorthodox recruiting methods of a kind, which at first sight have a startling hit-or-miss appearance. The danger of such methods lies in the very fact that they seem so divorced from calculated Secret Service machinations. Their slapdash appearance gives them a spurious aura of innocence.

The story of a young clerk, James Howard, provides an illustration of this.

Howard worked for a time in the West Country.

Shortly before he was due for a transfer to London, young Howard was idly reading the paper when he noticed a somewhat unusual advertisement. It had apparently been inserted by a foreigner living in London who was anxious to meet a young Englishman with a view to playing tennis.

Howard liked foreigners. He found them often more free and easy than his own countrymen. He replied – and in return received a letter from an address in Cadogan Gardens, London, as a result of which, a week before he was due to be transferred, Howard, the clerk, found himself being entertained in a local hotel by a Russian diplomat and his wife.

The diplomat was called Vasek.

Howard was discreetly questioned during a copiously expensive meal about his background, relatives, and education. When the evening was over, the diplomat Vasek knew for certain that Howard was a man ripe for worthwhile cultivation.

He was employed in a civilian capacity in an establishment connected with a department of the armed forces. Because Vasek had a heavy accent, to anyone connected in any way to the forces of the Crown or indeed any government department this should have sent alarm bells banging louder than Big Ben at midnight. He may have been only a clerk but in Vasek's eyes he was a clerk with a difference. So, on 4th December 1957, the usual "friendship" began, with its inevitable round of discreet dinners, visits to the cinema and theatre – and tennis or plans for tennis when the weather permitted.

But on this occasion Vasek had a short run.

On the morning of the 12th March 1958, Vasek and his wife were observed to leave home by car. More important, they were taking measures that were obviously intended to elude anybody who might be trying to follow them.

They did not succeed.

At the Bond Street Underground Station the security men saw Vasek meet a young man, take him to a cinema, then to dinner in Chelsea, and then to his home in West London. The next morning James Howard was followed to work.

Now the security machinery got to work on a broad front.

The following steps were taken:

1. Consultation with Howard's department revealed him to be a clerical officer aged 23, who would not normally, himself, handle secret material, but whose duties allowed him into rooms where such material was handled by others.
2. A number of his friends were discreetly investigated. They appeared to be of no security interest, though Howard later admitted that, as he put it, they were "unorthodox from the point of view of sex".
3. Observation was naturally continued on Howard himself. On 15th April, he was seen to visit Vasek's home carrying a well-filled briefcase – a briefcase that he had carried on previous occasions.
4. Finally in this particular case, it was decided that prevention was better than cure – and possible punishment.
5. Howard was interviewed, the social approach technique was explained, and he promised to see no more of Vasek. In the end Howard did not keep his promise. The social entertainment and perks of his treacherous trade proved too strong an attraction.

But now ironically, Vasek became almost as disillusioned with Howard as the security authorities.

Here is what happened:

At one stage Howard had told Vasek that he was bored with his job and underpaid. Vasek, alarmed at future prospects or perhaps lack of them – urged him to be patient. But by June, Howard had left Crown employment and taken a job in commerce. This was bad, from Vasek's point of view.

Worse was the fact that Howard did not tell him.

Vasek only found out by chance and from now on he regarded Howard as a useless and unreliable investment. Slowly and tactfully he began to disengage himself from this unprofitable, time-wasting, and irritating venture.

James Howard's whirl in diplomatic circles was over. This grooming happens today.

How Conceit Works

No harm, as far as is known, was done to national interests, but the above case is of note for the following reasons:

A. Vasek, with his advertisement, flung his not very attractive bait into a wide sea – and got a bite of the kind he wished.
B. Howard, when questioned, admitted he had seen a written instruction to report to his employers any contacts or peripheral approaches made to him by Russian or other hostile intelligence agencies.
C. He considered it "a piece of monstrous impertinence, the worst type of bureaucratic nonsense".
D. He said he knew Vasek to be as "straight as a die".
E. He considered he was capable of looking after himself.
F. He clearly was not capable of looking after himself. Given half a chance, he would doubtless have fallen into the first real trap Vasek set for him, homosexual or otherwise.
G. He must, at the very least, have had certain suspicions about Vasek's interests and ultimate intentions, since he tried to deceive him when he left the crown service. He wanted, in fact, a few of the lesser fruits of espionage without the risks of spying.

H. He thought he could in some measure double-cross an experienced, hostile intelligence officer.

James Howard was wrong all along the line.

It may be unnecessary to add that Vasek said that one reason for getting to know Howard was to learn about the British way of life with the aid of ordinary British people: the voice was the voice of Vasek, but the threadbare old excuse recalls that of his superior officer – none other than the patient Colonel Novak, of the Lloyd case, whom we have already watched at work.

The purpose of all these briefings is to bring to mind to all people in positions of trust the sheer scale of the spy-grooming problem we must be continually watchful and on guard against in Britain today, especially as we move into a theatre of what is almost certainly a new cold war.

So far it has been music and tennis. The story I will tell you now is football.

Nikolai Kicks Off

If not just a great actor, then Nikolai was certainly the genuine article, which in these pages means that he was a Russian Intelligence Officer.

This implies, in turn, that every time he met somebody abroad he asked of himself, "Can this person help me? If so, how can I get to know him better, and make him work for me?"

One September evening, Nikolai went into a public house in the Shepherd's Bush district of London. In an ingenuous sort of way he asked a man drinking by himself what he, as a foreigner should order.

We do not know, and probably never will know, whether Nikolai approached the stranger as a result of some very careful talent-spotting operation or whether, on the principle that one has to start somewhere, he was just employing hit-or-miss tactics. If the latter, he was very lucky indeed.

The stranger was Sergeant Brown, an army clerk working in the then War Office, now the Ministry of Defence.

We may as well say at once that when he had given his own name to the sergeant, Nikolai expressed a keen desire to understand the British way of life and how ordinary people spend their leisure.

At that time during the first cold war, however much the security authorities may have heard of this worthy and apparently widespread desire among Russian diplomatic staff, it sounded reasonable enough to the simple sergeant, who chatted away happily and mentioned among other things, that he played for the War Office Football Team.

Nikolai may or may not have been interested in sport, in general, or football in particular. If he wasn't, he clearly had to be, and without delay.

In the fullness of time, Nikolai, officer of the Russian Intelligence Service, became a firm supporter of the British War Office Football Team!

For this hostile intelligence agency, it was a promising kick-off.

Nikolai Wins Friends

Nikolai, interpreter and clerk in the office of the Soviet Military Attaché, became quite popular with the team, especially with White, the captain, and Green, the secretary, who were civilian clerical officers.

He became even more popular in November when he contributed the drinks, including the inevitable bottle of vodka, at a party given at his suggestion in the flat of Sergeant Brown, and during the following months Nikolai industriously cemented his relationship with his little network of clerks.

He met them separately at agreed meeting places, such as Trafalgar Square, Marble Arch, and a favourite of Nikolai's was the south side of Waterloo Bridge where it is my belief he wanted to try to gain access to the social facilities of the Union Jack Club. He would, at this meeting place, frequently suggest a drink or two at the Wellington Bar next door to the UJC, which was always full of servicemen on leave. He entertained his new found friends individually to dinner and a cinema or theatre show. He gave them presents of gin, vodka and cigarettes.

On one occasion there was a hint of money in the air. He told the team captain, White, that he was collecting material for an innocuous article he was writing for a Soviet journal, and invited White to assist him. Further, he not only promised White a fee but offered to give it to him in advance.

The game was going well, in Nikolai's opinion.

There was just one thing wrong.

At the November party, a certain War Office staff sergeant thought it well to make a report of it, even though it seemed to be merely a pleasant cheerful evening.

As a result Sergeant Brown was interviewed. So was team captain White. They were warned of danger, told they could continue seeing Nikolai, but instructed to report any significant moves.

So, through the peripheral vigilance of a staff sergeant, and quite soon after the kick-off, Nikolai was offside though he didn't know it.

The danger had been contained through the sound common sense of one man who reported contact with a Russian official, even though – as James Howard had at first thought – the social relationship seemed harmless.

But there is no doubt that in the beginning the three clerks were amused and flattered and entertained by Nikolai's attention.

Of interest, too, was the incident of collecting material for a harmless article. This hoary old approach, leading to possible sinister but clever persuasion is almost as frequent as the so-called desire to get to know the British way of life by mixing with "ordinary people".

Both tactics can lead to disaster.

Both are easy to discern.

Let us now briefly observe a more delicate approach.

Miss Benson Regrets

In this very short story there are only two characters – and a lady's ring. But it shows an original and elastic mind at work.

Krasnov, an official at the London Embassy of one of Russia's allies, was good-looking and pleasant. He spoke excellent English.

He was well fitted for the role he had to fill.

His target: Miss Benson, secretary of a Member of Parliament.

His mission: She might see documents summarising Western views on certain current political issues.

He had met her in the course of the social life which forms part of all political and diplomatic activity, and it may well be that he really liked Miss Benson. In view of Krasnov's attractive personality, it would certainly not be surprising if Miss Benson liked Krasnov.

Be that as it may, in the fullness of time a friendship developed between them, and in the fullness of time too, the Member of Parliament went abroad for a while, leaving Miss Benson to look after his affairs.

It is interesting and instructive to watch how from now on this man and this woman, who may well have been good friends, put personal considerations aside and reacted each according to the basic demands of the duties they were carrying out and the common sense they both possessed.

For Krasnov, the absence of the Member of Parliament was a golden opportunity. It was his big chance.

One day he casually remarked that Members of Parliament must surely be interested and well informed on topical, political matters. He, too, was interested in such matters. Surely Miss Benson must be in a position to see documents on this subject?

Miss Benson discreetly replied that it was almost impossible for her to obtain such documents.

For Krasnov this was discouraging; but he did not consider the position hopeless. After all, Miss Benson had, perhaps deliberately, in his view, used the word "almost".

Krasnov was now faced with a problem. As an intelligent man he had rightly judged that a crude offer of money, as an opening gambit, would be worse than useless to a person of Miss Benson's character.

He solved the problem to his own satisfaction by seeking Miss Benson's advice in the little matter of choosing a ring to send home as a present to his wife.

Miss Benson was not particularly surprised when she herself received a ring worth £20 a few days later.

Sometimes spies escape, such as the late Guy Burgess (left) and Donald McLean (right), one-time Foreign Office diplomats, who fled to Russia.

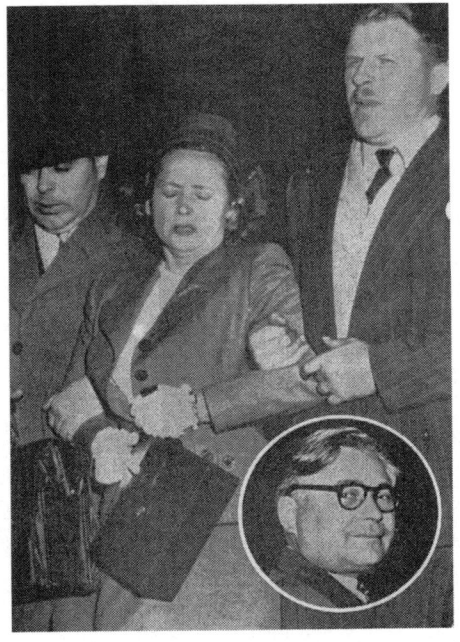

These people fled from the Russians. Armed Soviet agents attempting to take Madame Petrov back to the U.S.S.R. after the defection of her diplomat husband, Vladmir (inset). When their plane re-fuelled at Darwin, M.Petrov sought political asylum in Australia.

John Vassall (above), the Admiralty spy (18 years), and George Blake (below), formerly of the Foreign Office (42 years).

Another atomic scientist, Dr. Klaus Fuchs, also betrayed his country (14 years).

Espionage is nothing new. But in recent decades events have revealed that Communist Intelligence services have intensified their efforts to obtain classified information from sources in Britain. How many spies are operating in Britain no one can say. But this is known: From 1946 to 1962 eleven persons received prison sentences for offences under the Official Secrets Acts. Photographs of some of the convicted are given on these pages. They present what are ostensibly ordinary, harmless people. But their records of treachery stress that at no time can we relax in striving to keep our secrets secret.

Harry Houghton and Ethel Gee sold naval secrets (15 years).

Because he was an 'illegal' spy master, Conon Molody alias Gordon Lonsdale lacked the protection of diplomatic immunity (25 years), but he was eventually exchanged for Greville Wynne.

Peter and Helen Cohen alias Kroger, sought for years by the F.B.I., who were finally caught in Britain (20 years each).

Neither were the security authorities surprised, to which she had by now, with common sense and acumen, reported all the circumstances.

Miss Benson returned the ring, expressing her polite regrets that it was impossible in her position, to accept a gift.

Thus, the affair began and ended with delicacy and good manners on both sides, and the courtesies were at all times maintained.

For Krasnov, the return of the ring was the end, if not of a long and beautiful relationship, at least of a short and hopeful one.

They did not meet again.

The Russians have a phrase for incidents such as these:

"The scythe has struck a stone".

The Lonely Dutchman

There was nothing at all delicate, at least at one stage, in the methods used to suborn George Reynolds, a 19-year-old National Service member of the Royal Air Force, as will be shown in this story.

The enemy Intelligence Services spend much time and money talent spotting among those serving with the British Armed Forces. We have already seen Nikolai at work with the three war office clerks. Let us now look at this case in which an RAF man was involved.

George Reynolds' time came one Sunday in May 1957 but it could be one Sunday in May 2010 for as mentioned before, spying, like prostitution is ageless and so basic that great change is seldom necessary – remember – "If it ain't broke, don't fix it"!

Reynolds' duties in the RAF were those of a tape relay operator, passing messages in code and plain language. But on the Sunday in question he was on leave.

Wearing his RAF uniform, no doubt partly because it was easier to get a lift in uniform, he was patiently waiting by the roadside until a car should stop and help him on his way to London from his station at Newmarket.

In London, his wife waited, little knowing that when a car did stop, it would involve her husband in trouble of which she herself would have no inkling.

Come to that, Reynolds didn't know it himself, of course – not at first, and by the time he did know it, it was too late for one of his weak character.

Yet had anybody asked Reynolds, that morning in May, whether he was capable of 'looking after himself', there is no doubt that, like James Howard, he would have indignantly answered in the affirmative.

Certainly there was nothing suspicious, at least to Reynolds, about the friendly Dutchman who stopped for him.

What could be more harmless than a Dutch Commercial Salesman, calling himself Marek, a man who in the general exchange of chat about jobs said that he himself was, in a sense, interested in transmissions, since he sold radios and teleprinters? A 'bond in common', so to speak.

Furthermore, the Dutchman said he was lonely. He had few friends in England, poor chap. So when Marek suggested that Reynolds and his wife might like to dine with him in London, it seemed almost a kindness to accept. If not a kindness, at least it would be a free meal.

The only trouble was:

- A. Marek was not a Dutchman
- B. Marek was not a salesman
- C. Marek was certainly not lonely. He was a Russian diplomat and spy, had many acquaintances, and the full power of a hostile Intelligence Service to call on.

Temporary Dividends

In the end, Reynolds and his wife had quite a few free meals – about five or six, by the end of July 1957. Marek even made George Reynolds a member of a London club, and, what is more, paid his subscription for him in full.

Marek also gave the Reynolds a television set. It was a used one. This might have been subtlety on the grounds that a new set might seem too much of a good thing, whereas a used set, from a man in the business, could be understandable. On the other hand, we must face the fact that it might have been just a prudent measure of economy.

Still, for Reynolds the business of helping a lonely Dutchman was paying good dividends, one way and another.

The crunch was bound to come.

The first hint of it occurred at a lunch between Marek and Reynolds, by themselves in August.

Here the usual old gambit of offering money in exchange for harmless catalogues and brochures was cleverly and surprisingly reversed.

Marek had the literature; but he claimed he could not understand it.

Neither, as it happened could Reynolds; nor, Reynolds pointed out, did they have a technical reference library at his unit headquarters.

This was only a momentary setback for Marek. Indeed, in view of his long-term plans, it was hardly a setback at all, because unfortunately Reynolds now had a bright idea.

He remembered he had at home some notebooks dating from the time of his RAF training. Anxious, in some way, to repay his lonely but generous Dutch friend, he promised to lend the notebooks to Marek some time.

Then accompanied by his wife, Reynolds went happily on holiday.

The Grateful Victim

Marek was happy too, he had reason to be. His hospitality and gifts had clearly created in Reynolds a sense of obligation that could lead to a rosy future.

These initial tactics, these preliminary steps of making a potential victim feel grateful, were well known to Marek, the spy. They often bought fine results in the end. They might succeed now.

They did.

They succeeded so well that on his return from holiday, possibly eager to help his good friend Marek, and almost certainly eager for some more free meals, Reynolds went so far as to search diligently for Marek at various drinking clubs until he found him.

So Marek didn't need to chase Reynolds now. Reynolds was chasing him. His victim was running towards him, and eagerly too.

However, when he invited Reynolds and his wife out to dinner again, and arranged to pick them up by car, he did casually remind Reynolds about the technical notebooks.

After all, one might as well make sure about things.

In the car that evening the two wives sat behind, the two men in front. In the car Reynolds discreetly slipped the notebooks on to the shelf beneath the dashboard. It was a furtive action, the first of many to come.

His wife did not see it. She was not meant to see it.

Often in the spy battle it is the innocent wives who suffer most when their husbands become creatures of the spy masters.

In early September, Marek decided that the time had come for the pay-off to begin in earnest. He had told Reynolds that he would return the notebooks to him in Newmarket, and in Newmarket he duly entertained Reynolds to dinner and drinks at an inn.

But he returned no notebooks.

Instead he suggested that they might drive to Epping Forest and have a quiet talk, and there, in a quiet clearing in the forest, a dramatic little scene took place.

The lonely Dutchman dropped his disguise.

He asked Reynolds point blank to collaborate with him in obtaining secret information.

Reynolds refused.

Marek was ready for this. He pointed out, no doubt in as nice a way as possible, that by handing over his notebooks Reynolds had placed himself in what could be called a difficult position. He had crossed that line into "Dragonland". The door of the bear trap was about to drop. It was naked blackmail now.

Marek added, perhaps to discourage any ideas of violence, that in fact, the notebooks were hidden somewhere else in the forest. So they were.

In the event, Marek returned them, there was no reason why he shouldn't. As he pointed out ominously to Reynolds, he was retaining photographic copies of them. Then came the ultimate insult.

He gave Reynolds one pound for his taxi fare back to London. The airman went by underground and kept the change.

Well, in real life let's face it, did he really expect an expensive watch, a Bentley Continental, a Learjet to exotic beaches or a private tailor in Rome! The truth is, the "Spy Game" then, as it is today is notoriously unrewarding and dangerous. It never was, and is not today, at all a "James Bond" lifestyle.

Reynolds pleaded for a period in which to think it over. He had made up his mind by the time they met again, this time in Clapham.

He agreed. He was flat on the floor inside the bear trap. Well and truly hooked.

From now on, the case assumed a familiar pattern, at least in some respects.

Clandestine methods of communication were employed so that when Reynolds wished for a meeting he was to make a mark against a letter A in a telephone box, (pre-1980 phone system).

A dead letter box was arranged where Reynolds could leave material of possible interest to Marek; and again the telephone directory was used to indicate the time and date when material would be there.

In return for his traffic in treason Reynolds received several hundred pounds. One payment was for as much as £150, in one-pound notes, to enable Reynolds to make a deposit on a flat.

Indeed, compared to the value of information supplied by Lloyd, the electronics engineer, and Lloyd's potentialities, Reynolds was well rewarded for his treachery.

He would doubtless have been even better rewarded, had he agreed to stay in the RAF when his National Service had finished.

As an earnest of better things, Marek offered him £300 down if he would stay on.

But Reynolds refused absolutely.

He had several hundred pounds, a deposit on a flat, a great deal of hospitality – and a used television set. Perhaps he thought that enough was as good as a feast, at least in the RAF sphere.

Marek discussed with him the various possibilities in civilian W/T communication, where he might continue his secret activities, but it is perhaps significant that the next time they met was the last. It was on 2nd May 1958, and Reynolds' service in the RAF was finished.

At this meeting, Marek said that his own period of service – in Britain – was also coming to an end.

He went through the motions at least, of arranging how his successor would get in touch with Reynolds, if he so wished:

- A. Reynolds would receive a postcard from a person with a fictitious name. The postcard would be posted in Paris.
- B. Reynolds would then suggest a time and date for a meeting, in a telephone directory.
- C. Subsequently, he would walk round a block of buildings, be approached by a stranger, and mutual identifications would be established by an innocent question and answer, which Marek then gave him.

It appears that no postcard ever came from Paris.

Possibly the arrangements were made in earnest. Possibly, for Marek, or his successor, having discussed matters with their Centre, decided that Reynolds had outlived his usefulness and should be tactfully discarded.

As far as the security authorities in Britain were concerned, Reynolds had certainly outlived his usefulness. He naturally thought that he had escaped observation.

He was wrong.

He had been under investigation for some months. Early in 1959 the case having progressed no further, he was interrogated.

Marek had foreseen this possibility and at their last meeting he had warned Reynolds what to do if it happened.

- A. He should readily admit friendship.
- B. He should steadily deny passing information.

So, perhaps there was a third possible reason why no postcard came from Paris. Maybe Marek thought the authorities were suspicious.

At his interrogation, Reynolds adhered strictly to Marek's instructions. But at length he told the truth, and it was possible to fill in the details of the story of "Marek, the lonely Dutchman".

The Approach From Abroad

Hostages of fate, a hackneyed enough title, is unfortunately exactly appropriate to a threat already mentioned earlier in these pages.

The threat is based upon a brutal exploitation of human love and affection. It has its roots in distant lands but its tentacles reach unwillingly both for our secrets and for other information. The word "unwillingly" is used because in most cases it probably represents the true state of mind of the émigrés who are involved.

The émigrés concerned are usually people who have left their homeland because they would not tolerate life under a Communist or Dictatorial Government or regime. Clearly, they would not normally wish to do anything that would help that government.

Sometimes they feel they must. They have little choice.

The compulsion stems from the relatives they have been separated from by fate in the shape if world affairs.

One day a man may come to them and say: "Unless you do what I wish, unless you spy for me, things could go badly wrong for your relatives back home – and you know what that means."

The blackmail is hard to resist.

The Hidden Risks

The dangers of this and to this type of émigré are as follows:

A. The fact that true, political émigrés inevitably, and rightly, arouse in this country a certain feeling of sympathy.

B. Some of them may arouse personal recollections of the time when they or their compatriots were comrades in arms.

C. Since they have fled from Dictatorships or declined to return to their own Communist-ruled country, with all that that implies in the way of exile, there is an inclination to think they must be "all right" from the security angle.

And so most of them are.

Reluctantly, however, it is necessary to regard with great caution every émigré who still has relatives in Russia or in the former or present lands of her allies, or indeed, any other unsavoury dictatorship. This includes the ones we continue, for some unfathomable reason, to arm and bankroll on a year-by-year basis, even today.

In protecting ourselves we are ultimately protecting the émigrés and their relatives.

Sometimes the émigré is used to try to gain information about state secrets, but sometimes he can be used in quite a different capacity, as the following two stories show.

In order to understand what is behind them, it is necessary to appreciate that every émigré from, let's say a Communist regime, is a very bad advertisement for Communism indeed.

Many émigrés, especially Russians, have strong emotional ties with the mother country. To just sever them rather than live under Communism represents a slap in the face to which Communist governments are even more sensitive than they are about most things, which is to say a good deal.

Such governments take an unhealthy interest in their émigrés – unhealthy, that is, for the émigrés – and try to learn as much as possible about them.

If they can entice them, to renounce life under Western democracy and return home, so much the better.

They also regard them, sometimes with reason, as centres of intrigue and anti-communist propaganda. In short:

- A. Communist or dictatorial governments don't like émigrés.
- B. Communist or dictatorial governments want to know all there is to know about them – and take steps to find out. Covert and overt patience is their calling card.

The Lost Sheep

A convenient stepping-stone in such matters, for the old Rumanian government, in the opinion of Mr Andreas, the diplomat and intelligence officer, was a certain Mrs Mayfield, of his nationality but wife of a British subject. She was convenient for three reasons:

1. She had an old mother at home.
2. She wanted to bring her old mother to England, which then necessitated an exit visa.
3. She had worked at one time for the Foreign Office and the BBC, and knew quite a number of émigrés from her own country. A perfect subject for grooming. The chance was not one to be missed.

And so began the art of deception when one day, after she had duly applied for an exit visa for her mother, Mrs Mayfield, much to her surprise, found Mr Andreas from the legation on her doorstep.

Mr Andreas seemed in an affable and helpful mood.

He said that pending the possible grant of an exit visa for the old mother, Mr and Mrs Mayfield might like to visit her; in which case he, benevolent Mr Andreas, could help with visas for them; or they might care to send her parcels of certain commodities which she could sell on the Black Market and thereby improve her living conditions.

All he wanted in return was a flow of information about émigrés in Britain.

Mrs Mayfield declined to help.

When it was pointed out by Andreas, no longer so affable, that her obstinacy might have the most unfavourable consequences for her mother, Mrs Mayfield's dilemma must have been acute and painful. Perhaps she had always expected such a day to arrive, perhaps she had long since decided upon her attitude in the face of such sordid blackmail.

She remained firm.

In this case, the story has a happy ending. Mrs Mayfield's courageous defiance cost her nothing.

Her mother obtained her exit visa and came to England – though not, one may be sure, as a result of any helpful action by the frustrated Mr Andreas.

The probable explanation is that Andreas heard of the visa application through his official position and decided upon a personal ploy, an off the cuff blackmail action which, eventually, had only one result for him: He was declared "persona non grata"!

But had Mrs Mayfield's mother received parcels, sold the contents on the Black Market, and been arrested, the pressure could perhaps have become almost unbearable, even for Mrs Mayfield.

Black market blackmail is not uncommon and features in a later story, but first, we will glance at some activity among Russian émigrés.

In the autumn of 1955, the Soviet Government surprised the world by declaring amnesty for all categories of political refugees except those against whom war crimes could be proved.

This superficially broadminded gesture was not, of course, grounded in some form of concerned humanitarianism, but was designed to lure back to Russia those groups of refugees whose continued residence abroad was, at least, a source of political embarrassment to the Soviet Government.

A result of the amnesty was that the Russian Consular Authorities tried to learn even more than usual about their émigrés, both as groups and as individuals.

What I tell you next is a fair example of the sort of thing that happened.

One day in 1956, a Soviet consular clerk arrived in this country. His duties seemed innocuous. They were concerned with travel bookings, and arrangements to supply visas for embassy and trade delegation officials and for people wishing to visit Russia. He also had to supervise the arrivals and departures of Russian ships from the Port of London and maintain contact with British shipping agents.

He had, however, another duty that did not become immediately apparent.

It became apparent when one day a frightened Baltic refugee called Jonas Vilnis sought the help of the British police.

Jonas Vilnis had an interesting tale to tell.

As in our previous case of Mrs Mayfield, Vilnis had had a caller. But whereas Mrs Mayfield's caller had been from a satellite legation, this visitor said he was from the Soviet Foreign Office itself.

It was the Consular Clerk, using a false name – and armed with a letter from a friend of Vilnis who was still in the Soviet Union.

The Consular Clerk wanted four things:
1. Information about fellow émigrés.
2. Names and addresses of subscribers to the particular émigré newspaper in which Vilnis was interested.
3. Names and addresses of other Balts in this country to whom the Embassy could send copies of a Russian paper printed in their own particular language.
4. Name and address of somebody who might be willing to return to his homeland, and later re-enter Britain, allegedly to make propaganda.

Under one guise or another and for whatever purpose, revealed or unrevealed, the demands mostly boiled down to an operation with a single aim – to obtain information about émigrés groups and personalities in this country.

Jonas Vilnis saw clearly the danger of being groomed in such a way, declined to assist, and, as stated, went to the police for help and advice. He knew it was the only right and sensible thing to do.

It soon became apparent that blatant bullying and the grossest intimidations were being employed by certain Russian officials. This was not only intolerable to public opinion but also against the laws of this country. The Russians were officially warned that further actions of this kind would not be permitted. The activities ceased – at least openly.

Such crude methods as those employed by the Russians and their allies are far removed from their normal subtlety, and can hardly be regarded as intelligence work.

But they illustrate that though they may think themselves secure, political refugees are never quite beyond the reach of their governments.

Stalking The Duck

Before we leave this subject, however, it is worthwhile to note how hostile intelligence services can employ exactly opposite methods to those described above – not threats or blackmail, that is, but the technique of The Lure.

Here we will see an example of how this deceptive little ploy can work.

In this case history, Vladislav Gorski, the Polish civilian barber, began it all, though in an innocent enough way – he happened to be employed at an RAF station near Bath. This was Poland pre-1989.

Gorski was a curious mixture, in that although an émigré he had chosen to retain his Polish nationality. He was therefore, not perhaps an ideal choice, on form, for a job at an RAF base, but if the Polish Intelligence Service ever had any vague idea of coercing the humble hairdresser they soon had more important prey in sight.

Gorski became a mere stepping-stone to more ambitious plans.

He inadvertently became a stepping-stone when, in the fullness of time, he applied to the Polish Embassy for a passport to visit his son in Poland, and arrange, if possible for the young man to join him in England.

The passport, perhaps to Gorski's surprise was granted.

Doubtless, one fact had escaped his attention: when applying for a passport he had been obliged to state where he was employed.

Nevertheless, nothing happened to Gorski, The Barber, when he went to Poland, and in due course he happily returned to his barbering.

Then one day he received a visit, and the visitor, calling ostensibly for social purposes, was none other than an official who had interviewed him at the Consul-General.

He was also, as it happened, a member of the Polish Intelligence Service.

As we talk of Poland here it is wise to remember this story was circa 1960.

Now luck played a part, or so it must have seemed to the Polish Intelligence Service. For Gorski, by chance, was at the time entertaining another Pole. The other Pole was called Zaremba. Whatever ideas the UB man may have had about Gorski, he must have speedily changed them.

It was not surprising.

Zaremba was a warrant officer attached to Fighter Command and had full knowledge of highly secret radar equipment.

Zaremba became the prey now. And as I mentioned before, one of the bedrocks of a good hostile intelligence agency has to be covert patience.

The Sitting Duck

Nothing happened for some months. Doubtless it took time, not only to evolve the plot, but also to get it approved by the Polish Centre. These things are not hurried.

Like all good plans the one chosen was a simple one, though but for another stroke of luck it might have required a long period to mature.

It began with a further visit to Gorski, but on this occasion by two officers of the military branch of the Polish Intelligence Service. Ostensibly, the visit was a social one, and if the simple barber was flattered it was only because he foolishly omitted to ask himself what he had to offer, apart perhaps from a free hair-cut, to two embassy officials.

What he had to offer was an introduction, some day soon, or otherwise, to the all-important Warrant Officer Zaremba.

This might have been long delayed, of course, had it not been for the fortunate coincidence that Zaremba was also visiting Gorski when the two officials called.

The intended but new victim was waiting on the premises.

The Polish Intelligence Service was in no hurry. Zaremba must not be made suspicious. Any instinctive hostility had to be overcome.

He had to be persuaded that Poland, even under Communism, was changing, growing more tolerant and liberal-minded, that even Communism, these days, could be human.

Presents of drinks and cigarettes helped. So did the convivial evenings enjoyed by the barber, the Warrant Officer, who had so many precious secrets in his head, and the two friendly embassy men.

All Poles are devoted to their homeland, and many nostalgic thoughts and memories must have drifted through the mind of Warrant Officer Zaremba, as the drink flowed, and the air grew thick with smoke, and the conversation was doubtless deftly turned by the Polish food and Polish customs – and distant friends and relations. It would be nice to see it all again – just for a short while, thought Zaremba.

Why not, they asked, why not go home for a visit?

But - what about a passport? Well, they could probably persuade the embassy to supply one. They might even persuade the embassy to help in various other ways.

We can see here how they were dropping morsels of food to entice the bird towards the cage trapdoor.

They went on, things have changed, they insisted and after all, friends must help each other. No good being in the embassy if you can't help a pal now and again, is it?

Both to Zaremba and also, without doubt to the Polish spies, it all seemed too good to be true.

It was.

As in the other case of Nikolai and the three war office clerks something went wrong.

The operation came within an ace of success. It would have succeeded completely but for the alertness of certain RAF officers who had been concerned about the friendship between Gorski, Zaremba and the Polish Visitors.

Gorski and Zaremba were interrogated.

The security dangers were explained.

Zaremba never went to Poland. He didn't want to go now.

He knew that landing in Poland with a Polish Passport, with no claim to any other status than that of a Polish citizen from the moment he set foot in that country, he would soon have been faced with a very simple question:

> "Tell us everything you know, whether you want to or not.
> And, if you don't want to, think again – or else."

Lucky Zaremba.

Beyond The Frontiers

On the whole, guile, patience and enticement are employed by enemy intelligence services operating in Britain and the Western world when recruiting agents. Their successful methods of yesteryear are in full flourish now, today, as you read this book of briefings, the tricks are working. Defects of character are sought, venality, idealism and innocence are exploited, together with deep-seated emotions such as fear, greed, sex, and panic caused by unexpected and difficult financial circumstances.

However distasteful such methods may seem, they are clever, delicate and gentlemanly compared with those that have been used against certain British citizens who were actually behind the Iron Curtain, particularly in Russia. Let us then, watch the Russian Intelligence Service at work on its own ground.

Here we will see it in its most crude, brutal, and sordid form.

Here we will see blackmailers at work unashamed, unabashed and inhuman.

Case No 1

Claude Robinson was a man who liked the Russians and may have done later on, though in view of what happened to him in Moscow, his liking was doubtless mingled with certain reservations.

He was particularly interested in promoting student group exchanges between this country and the Soviet Union and, in the fullness of time, found himself being entertained one evening by some Russian acquaintances, at the Restaurant Moskva in the Soviet capital.

There is an old Russian custom, which calls for frequent individual toasts across the table. There is a further rigid custom connected with the said custom: vodka glasses must be emptied at a gulp.

Claude gulped a great deal.

When he was semi-conscious he was helped to a bedroom. He was undressed. He was subjected to a homosexual assault.

The whole incident was photographed.

This well-planned old ploy was absurdly easy for the experts in blackmail.

There is no doubt that when he was later shown the photographs, the aim was to convince him that it would be wise to agree to any Russian Intelligence suggestions put to him later.

The implied threat was a criminal prosecution, and, among other things, the end of the hobby he was so interested in – cultural work among young people.

Claude Robinson did the sensible thing. He went to the British Embassy, and his early return to Britain was promptly arranged. But why was Claude Robinson chosen with his harmless job in culture and student groups? Surely even the Russians were not interested in the secrets of British culture?

They were not.

They were interested in the students who made up the groups. Claude Robinson would have been recruited as a talent spotter, to identify students who – perhaps if they later became civil servants or scientists – might possibly respond to carefully orchestrated Russian advances.

His role would not have been dramatic or spectacular but it would have been important. He might have been able to point to a future Fuchs, or Nunn May, or Vassall.

The problem raised was a difficult one.

It was impossible to tell a young man on a cultural exchange visit that he must decline all hospitality, even when it is offered in a public restaurant.

The Russians got round this by usually moving in groups of three or four.

The only other real defence was (A) knowledge of what may happen, and (B) knowledge of what to do if it did happen.

Case No 2

James Ford was of interest because the Russians had to try three different baits before they trapped him.

Ford was a newspaper correspondent in Berlin, and in Berlin, in due course, a Russian official came quietly to him one day and offered him generous and tempting payments for copies of the agency service messages.

The argument was doubtless plausible enough. What harm in letting them see material destined in any case for publication? Nothing secret. No risk to James Ford, just good money for easy work. Were his alarm bells about to sound?

But the Russians knew that such communications often contain background material that for security, patriotic or other reasons would never see the light of day in a newspaper. James Ford knew this, too, of course.

He firmly refused the offer.

He refused it at first in Moscow, also, where he was posted later, though there the bait was different.

It first appeared in the form of two attractive young ladies. They had no appeal for him. Why was this?

Perhaps the Russians had not done their homework properly, or perhaps the delving into his past life had only now been completed. At any rate, they tried a third time with a still different enticement.

This time they succeeded. A hidden camera provided the necessary evidence of a homosexual relationship with a Russian.

James Ford listened to the blackmail threat that was inevitably produced.

Claude Robinson could claim that he had been the victim of a frame-up. For James Ford it was different. He had acted voluntarily.

It must have required clear thinking and considerable moral courage to do what he did but it was the right thing to do without delay.

Like Robinson, he went to the embassy and told his story. A return to England was the only solution.

It was embarrassing, it was humiliating. But he had at least saved himself from the deep black and dangerous mire of espionage, and consequences which could have been very much worse than a return home from Moscow.

Case No 3

Frank Williams's case was quite different. He, most certainly, was a target worth aiming at. During those first Cold War years of which we speak, Williams was what they called Security Guard to the Queen's

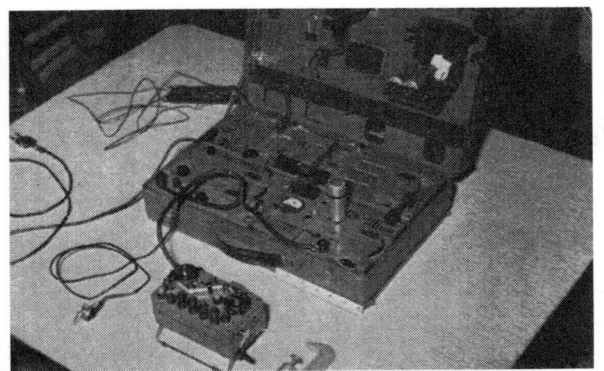

With the transceiver were two identical photographic prints giving a series of settings for the controls of the equipment against a series of three-figure numbers. This indicated that the equipment had been calibrated to transmit and receive at certain frequencies according to the three-figure number selected (top). In one of the packages was a tape-sender (seen in the foreground) using magnetic tape for high speed transmission of short messages. In other parts of the bungalow were found many other devices of the spy, including this cipher pad (bottom) which was used in the coding and decoding of messages.

Plugged into the back of a radiogram in the living-room was an aerial which, leading through the ceiling, was stapled round the sides of the loft. A switch cut out the loudspeaker when it was used as an external loudspeaker. This fitting, incidentally, was similar to one found on the wireless in Lonsdale's London flat. A pair of headphones, normally hidden behind the radiogram, were plugged into a pair of terminals to which a tape recorder found in Kroger's study could also be connected. The equipment was capable of receiving and recording messages, sent by voice or Morse code, from anywhere in the world.

The cache under the kitchen floor also revealed – apart from six thousand American dollars, two lenses which could have been used for making microdots, and other items – a miniature camera (top) and a casette with twelve frames exposed and two reloads. In the second drawer of the kitchen unit (bottom) was a plastic container holding magnetic iron oxide powder used as a visual aid to reading Morse signals recorded on magnetic tape. Other chemicals, plus photographic equipment, were found in the loft.

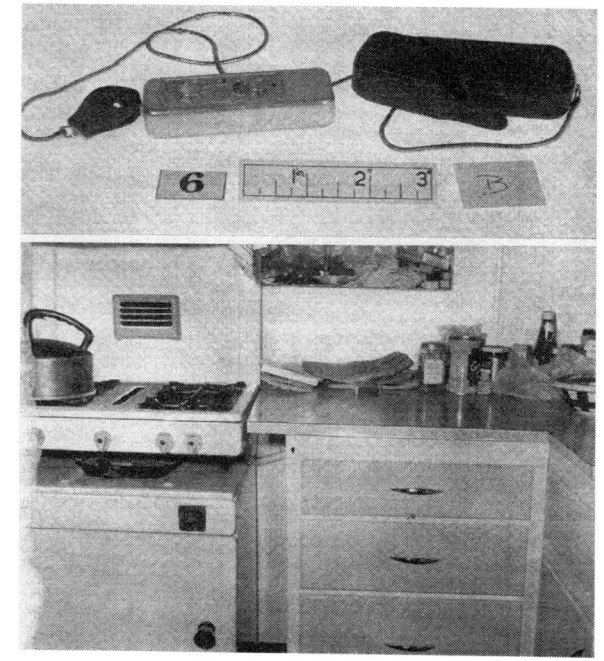

A table lighter (top) in the living-room had a secret hiding place similar to one found in Lonsdale's flat. It contained a one-time pad with a red printing partially used, two complete miniature pads with black printing, a miniature negative and two miniature prints of wireless transmission schedules. The top of a talcum tin in the bathroom unscrewed, revealing two secret compartments. One of these contained a microdot reader (bottom). Fittings in the bathroom showed that it was used as a photographic darkroom.

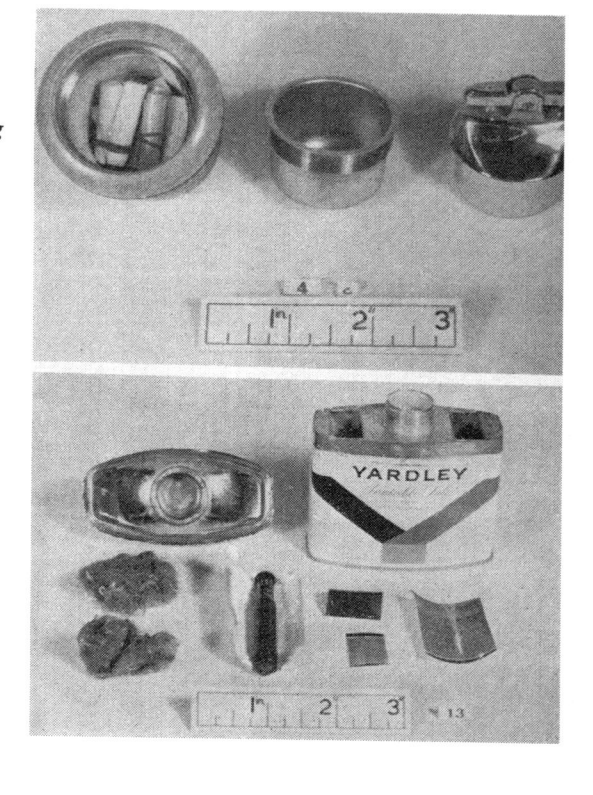

Probing the rubble beneath the kitchen floorboards, they located a secret cache (right) containing Polythene-wrapped radio and other equipment. In a plastic shopping-bag was a wireless transceiver fitted with a single earpiece (below).

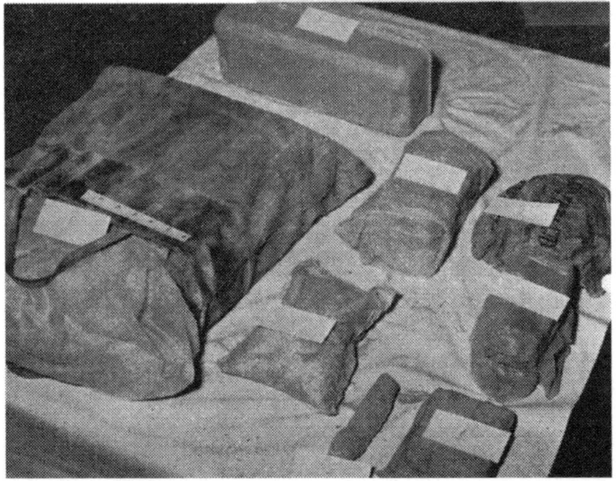

Communist Intelligence services are constantly trying to penetrate Britain's security screen to get at national secrets. Typical of this ceaseless campaign were the activities of Gordon Lonsdale, a Russian, whose real name is Conon Trofimovich Molody. This 'illegal' spy master controlled two spies in the Admiralty Underwater Detection Establishment and Portland, Harry Houghton and Ethel Gee. Also in his network were the American Communists, Peter and Helen Kroger, whose real name was Cohen. No passer-by would have suspected that their bungalow was a centre of espionage. Yet security men discovered otherwise.

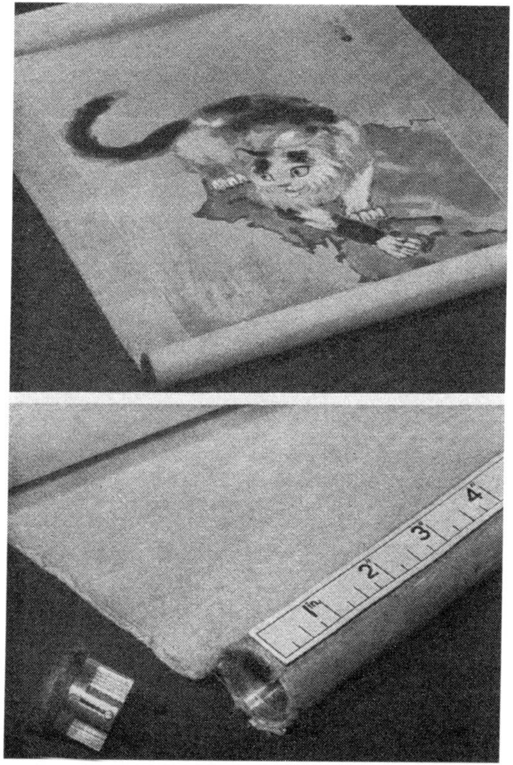

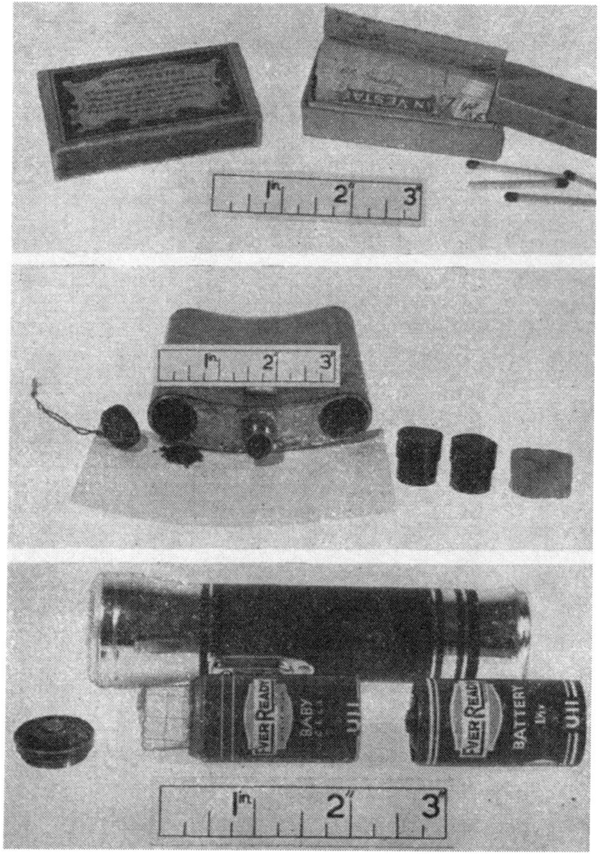

An innocent-looking box of matches (top), owned by Houghton, had a false bottom and was used as a hiding place. The note illustrated refers to arrangements for Houghton's meetings with a Russian Intelligence officer. The hip flask with two secret hiding places containing magnetic iron oxide powder (centre) was found in the Krogers' bungalow. The electric torch (bottom) with two battery cells, one of which was hollow, was in Lonsdale's flat and is identical with one found in the Krogers' bedroom.

Lonsdale's flat also proved to be a mine of espionage gadgets, including this Chinese scroll which hung over his bed. The bottom roller was a hollow metal tube and contained a quantity of American dollar bills.

Messenger, no less, who carried the diplomatic bag with its secrets, between Moscow and Berlin.

Even today, no target in intelligence, provided the potential gains are sufficient, is dismissed as impossible by the Russians and their allies, or other hostile agencies, and in this case the contents of the bag carried by the Queen's Messenger was a prize worthy of a major effort.

All they needed was possession of the bag for a comparatively short time, because to properly equipped experts the opening of a diplomatic bag and the photographing of the contents presented no insuperable difficulties.

For a long time the agents of the Russian intelligence service discreetly observed the routine followed by the Queen's Messenger and his guard in their journeys to and from Moscow and Berlin.

Finally they pinpointed a time and place which offered the opportunities they sought. It was during a halt at an airport.

Here, all things being well, it might be possible to spirit the real bag away and substitute a replica for a short while.

This operation could be done not just once but perhaps every time a journey was made. The reward would be a golden harvest in the form of continuous intelligence.

The secret observations revealed that the only snag in the way was Frank Williams.

Frank Williams had to agree to look the other way for a few seconds.

Some considerable time was spent by the Russians, in observing the habits of the stalwart, Frank Williams and trying to assess his character.

It was all most disappointing.

Frank was clearly a man who was very loyal to his country. Worse, he had no obvious vices to exploit.

Then when the problem seemed too baffling to be solved, a minor piece of information came to hand.

Frank Williams's Error

Many people, quite ordinary people, such as tourists, think the customs are fair game, a mildly exciting challenge to their nerve and ingenuity.

Frank Williams was one of them.

During his round trips he had sometimes indulged in some petty smuggling, for one thing, it probably relieved the tedium. It never amounted to much, hardly enough for a prosecution, certainly not enough for blackmail.

But it provided the key that the Russians were seeking.

One day in Moscow, Frank Williams received a telephone call from a man with an American accent. No, said the voice, they had never met, but he had often seen Mr Williams and knew that he regularly went to Berlin. Could Mr Williams possibly take some German films to Berlin for developing and printing?

Could they perhaps meet? Could Mr Williams call at his flat?

He could and he did.

Frank Williams was suspicious. When he arrived at the flat the general atmosphere and the refreshments did not seem very American.

But the opening conversation was innocent enough, and the man had a bundle of American ten-dollar bills, which looked genuine. He even counted them and asked Frank Williams to check the total.

Frank obliged.

Perhaps he was wrong, he now thought perhaps the man was an American after all. Some Americans take a pleasure in living like the indigenous population.

Frank Williams discovered he had not been wrong when the man dropped his "American" mask and offered him a straight payment of 10,000 dollars to cooperate in the matter of the Queen's Messenger and the bag.

The threat came when Frank Williams indignantly refused.

Petty smuggling was one thing, it was pointed out. Currency smuggling was very different indeed. It was a very serious offence under Russian law.

Frank Williams had clearly been smuggling American currency. He had the opportunity and he had smuggled other things, hadn't he? Furthermore, they now had a photograph of him holding dollar bills to prove it. They had just taken one. Would he like some copies for the press?

Frank Williams said he must think it over, though he had no intention of submitting. He did the only sensible and right thing. He reported the whole position he was in to his superiors.

So, once again, the British Embassy had to listen to a story of attempted blackmail, and once again, a British subject had to be removed from the city.

This attempt at recruitment was a failure as were many others, so the stories can be told. But for those brave few who walked away, there may have been many more too weak and indifferent to resist the enticements of crossing the line into "Dragonland".

No one can say for certain, but I suspect the weak ones who traded in treachery could be compared to the mass of the iceberg that destroyed the *Titanic* while the brave few to come clean, no more than the jagged spur which tore open the hull of hostile intelligence agencies but also had to destroy themselves.

There are other cases where Russian blackmail succeeded, but where the spy was caught.

There must be still others where the Moscow men, even today, trapped their victims and still hold them, stories known only to the spy centre – and to its victims.

Dot-Dash-Dot Men

During the first Cold War, inevitably, such people as wireless operators in our embassies were regarded with a speculative eye by hostile intelligence agencies, for they possessed important information such as call-signs and frequencies.

No Russian intelligence officer worth his Siberian salt could do other than regard an operator in the British Diplomatic Wireless Service, as it was then, as a target worthy of the greatest effort.

One operator and his wife were drawn into social relationships with other Russians by an apparently harmless Russian occupying a non-confidential post in our Moscow Embassy.

The good natured British couple, perhaps conscious of the hospitality they were receiving, gave presents of clothing and other articles from Britain to their Russian friends.

This was fair enough. The trouble, and it could have been serious, arose when little by little the couple began to use such articles as a form of currency payment.

The black market blackmail trap was ready to be sprung. In due course it was.

But again the victim did not submit. Again, here was a man who explained his situation to the Embassy and, once more there was an issue of one-way tickets away from Moscow. Another man had chosen integrity and loyalty over perhaps many years in a prison cell.

Ill-met In Wandsworth

The above stories I have given you show a heartening resistance to blackmail. But, this next story of a young wireless operator called Henry Nicholls was very different.

No blackmail for Nicholls.

To this day it is not known for certain why Nicholls became a Soviet agent.

The story is simple – the background more interesting.

It all happened one day in April 1952 when a Soviet Embassy official, known to be a spy, set out to keep an appointment.

As is usual with these people, he spent several hours trying to throw off anybody who might be observing his movements.

Eventually, in the respectable suburb of Kingston, London, he met his man. The man was Henry Nicholls. Nicholls produced papers. The Russian took notes.

You could almost say that they were old friends, as they had met on at least six previous occasions.

But, they were only destined to meet twice more, because on the second occasion, in St George's Park, Wandsworth, they were arrested, and Nicholls was found to be carrying a wallet containing details in his own handwriting of call-signs, frequencies and other important Diplomatic Wireless Service information.

The Russian was sent home.

The Briton got four years in prison.

He was lucky, but openly declared in court the foolish stupidity of his actions whilst working in a position of trust within the "military" theatre.

In espionage the difference between being a diplomat and not being a diplomat would seem to be an unpleasant sojourn in prison – in this country.

When I said Nicholls was lucky with four years, what I meant was – in some countries, the difference can be months of misery, torture, and a bullet.

Why Did He Do It?

Henry Nicholls never provided a satisfactory explanation. But perhaps if we look at his character and career we may find an inkling of the truth.

Nicholls joined the Diplomatic Wireless Service, after leaving the Army, in 1948, two years later he was posted to Moscow.

There is no doubt that he was glad to go. For one thing, it seems likely that he was already interested in communism, and now he would be able to see it in action. He arrived in Russia enthusiastic for the adventure.

In Moscow, two things happened.

On the one hand, he was impressed by the efforts and ideals of the Russian people. In some ways, no doubt, his earlier interest in communism had already conditioned him to be thus impressed.

On the other hand, he was a misfit at his place of work at the Embassy.

He could not enter into the very restricted British society available to him. He was too introspective. He was too unsociable.

Moody, isolated by his own nature, and unhappy, his work deteriorated even to the point where a transfer was considered. Being young, any criticism of his work doubtless led to further resentment. Like an angst-filled teenager.

He was indeed ripe fruit for the Russian Intelligence Service.

Perhaps he was recruited during one of the frequent visits to Russian cinemas which became his outlet, or perhaps, and quite possibly, by one of the Russian women on the Embassy domestic staff. It was significant that he disappeared from the Embassy for most of the day when he was due to leave. Maybe he was saying a fond farewell, but maybe other things were said in addition. But one thing is for sure.

Sometime, somehow, somewhere, during his year's tour of duty, Henry Nicholls became a spy for Russia.

So looking at this in clear light what can we now, in hindsight, say?

Perhaps he did it for ideological reasons, or because he had a social chip on his shoulder. Maybe because the Russians really seemed to appreciate him, as well they might, while he felt his own countrymen did not, and it seems hard to blame them.

Possibly the explanation is even simpler.

It almost looks as if Henry Nicholls' dark, withdrawn, inhibited, and unfriendly nature had provided him with a readymade, built-in, do-it-yourself spy mentality. Something of the night about him.

Looking back at this today, I wonder if it is reasonable to ask whether or not this could, or should have been picked up by his immediate superiors.

Well, I would say that's an in-depth question which is perhaps much more important within today's training format than yesterday's and runs parallel with our unfortunate new climate of political extremism. Next time you take the tube – look around you!

How Do We Stand?

We have seen how the hostile spy machine is organised and we have watched it at work.

The assessment must be that it is subtle and brutal, as occasion demands, that it is of vast dimensions, and that its agents delve in wide and varied fields.

Now let us glance briefly at the other side of the picture.

Like all large and ruthless organisations it has its weaknesses.

There is no doubt that Russia expects results, and in the attempt to achieve them, especially in the recruitment of new agents, some of her talent spotters go astray.

Ordinary courtesies shown to a Russian official, or an interest, real or politely simulated, in Russian art or literature, or in conditions in that country, are all noted. Often the individual concerned, apparently for this reason alone, thereupon begins to figure in the records as a potential recruit or "unconscious" informant.

During the last Cold War let us look for a moment, (in hindsight and as a lesson for today) at some typical messages between Moscow and Canberra, Australia. They were included in the report of the Australian judicial inquiry produced after the Russian Intelligence Officer, Petrov, had defected and revealed all that he knew. It was plenty.

In this detailed report the judges clearly explained that many examples were found in the Petrov papers of the marking down for "study" of persons whose patriotism no one could question.

These messages gave good indications of the line of thought pursued by the MVD, as it was then called, and seemed to show either an inordinate degree of wishful thinking by the Moscow Centre, or an over-anxious desire to please on the part of the operators in the field:

"Jack Hook, President of the Sydney Trade Union of the Labour Council, Labour supporter, one of the leading members of the

Labour Party. He collaborates with the Communist Party. He holds progressive views. "K" considers "H" to be a man who deserves to be trusted" (p.152)

The symbol "K" stood for the Australian talent spotter who recommended Hook to the MVD though obviously anxious to please his Russian masters his accuracy left much to be desired since the Royal Commission were able to satisfy themselves – not only that Hook was positively anti-communist but also that he did not even know "K".

"Concerning McLean. In the Political Intelligence Department of External Affairs of Australia there works, with the rank of First Secretary, F.J. McLean..."

"According to Sadovnikov's description, McLean has access to secret documents, knows well many workers in the Department of External Affairs, attends diplomatic receptions and consorts with members of the diplomatic corps.

He treated our representatives in Canberra with respect, willingly accepted invitations, and attended receptions arranged by our diplomats in private apartments.

During discussions he explained dissatisfaction with the Menzies Government ... Furthermore, he is more talkative and frank when he is at a small gathering or at private receptions..."

"One of our trustworthy agents ... considers that he could and would supply valuable information ... should be skilfully and tactfully handled and be convinced that nothing that he will say will come to the knowledge of any other Australians ... It should also be taken into account that McLean has a large family and is badly off materially..." (pp 157–8)

Petrov never carried out this instruction because he discovered that McLean was in hospital, and likely to remain there for some time. But casual acceptance of slight hospitality, coupled with the financial problem of bringing up a large family, had proved sufficient to bring McLean within the talent-spotters' sights.

This type of miscalculation was not peculiar to the operations in Australia. It was also specifically noted in the Report of the Royal

Commission on Espionage in Canada, produced after the Russian cipher clerk, Gouzenko, had defected.

In the documentary evidence appeared the name of a Colonel in the Canadian Army whom the Russians regarded as a subject for study with the ultimate object of recruitment. In his evidence – which the judges accepted without any reservations – this colonel stated:

"They have misinterpreted our sincere endeavour both my wife's and mine, to have them feel at home in Canada, and to show them something of Canada life; but I am cured" (p.52)

Perhaps the centre puts too much pressure on her agents in the field, drives them too hard threatens them too much.

The result, whatever the cause, is that much work and money is expended to no purpose whatever.

Even so, the fact remains that the Russians and their allies were at that time, and certainly are today as you read this, forever on the lookout, forever probing and testing especially on the peripheries of our military both at home and abroad. Careless talk costing lives was not only true in the 1940s but very much more so today. And lest we take too much comfort from the above examples, let us note one more message from Moscow to Canberra:

"Concerning O'Sullivan in reply to your paragraph ... We regard the study of O'Sullivan as very full of promise ... It is essential to verify the data supplied by O'Sullivan about himself ... A verification is being carried out by us in England; we shall inform you of the outcome.

In order not to draw the attention of the counter-intelligence ... O'Sullivan should not be invited any more to the Embassy...

It is desirable that, when a suitable opportunity offers, you should ask him to compile for us a survey concerning the economic, political, and military penetration of Australia by America, with the inclusion of unofficial data. Warn O'Sullivan that his survey will not be published ... and that it is required by you for your personal use. Promise him that the time spent ... will be compensated by you...

We request you to inform us in detail in every letter concerning progress in the study and cultivation of O'Sullivan." (pp199–120)

In fact, Petrov did cultivate O'Sullivan a little further and the case might have held much promise since, in the following year, O'Sullivan was appointed Press Secretary to the Leader of the Opposition.

Before the date of this instruction O'Sullivan had, indeed already supplied to the Russians a report on 45 other journalists. The Australian authorities accepted this report as authentic but withheld it from the published evidence because of its scandalous nature.

It represented a major contribution in talent spotting.

During the period of the first Cold War there were weaknesses in addition to these noted in the field of talent spotting.

One was the mania of Moscow Centre to supervise the most minute detail from the distant Russian capital.

We have already observed that even street meeting places, dates, times, and other details were rigorously controlled from the Centre. So, I think it was inevitable that such remote control would lead to delays, queries, counter queries, and in the event of a sudden and necessary alteration of plans, to confusion, mistakes and dismay.

Looking at the human aspect of this I think a second weakness was almost unavoidable in such a large, monolithic heavily disciplined organisation.

There were and I'm sure there are today, bound to be frail human links, or links which were strong when they started, but for all avenues of circumstantial reason have weakened with the years and the labour in what is certainly a front line theatre of "civilian" conflict.

We all know human nature is flexible, human characters do not remain static. They are constantly changing for the better or the worse.

Even people in the Intelligence Services of Russia and her allies, and many other modern day dictatorial regimes are subject to emotions such as fear, resentment, greed, spite, an excess of strain, or a sudden political conversion.

Then one of the weak links may snap.

Then, let's say from Russia, there is a defector to the West, and the balloon goes up. Added to the dedicated efforts of our own security authorities the information brought over by a defector can be of inestimable value to the West and disastrous to our opponents. There have been quite a few.

Doubtless there will be more,

Finally, the spy has also to contend with the vigilance of our own population.

Despite certain lapses over the years the British people are a highly observant, suspicious, intelligent, and patriotic race.

No spy is safe, or should I say no spy was safe during the second great war or the first Cold War. Over the turn and into this new century too many people have retreated as though living and rolling around in one of those transparent space-balls that is their own private bunker. They really believe events around them are of no consequence to their "paint-by-numbers" well-ordered lives. I will try to analyse why in my conclusive comments later.

The Odds Against

The spy may listen to the comforting words of his spy master. He may soothe his nerves with recollections of the elaborate precautions taken to protect him, and flatter himself upon his guile.

A "spook", I believe that's the modern term, may elude for a period the attention of the security authorities and his watchful fellow citizens, since no spy can be caught until he has done some spying.

Yet, he must never forget in the long run, the odds are against him. For one thing, despite all the precautions, the cunning, and the ingenuity, he cannot protect himself against that weak link we talked about: The defector in his own organisation, and you can take that as from the horse's mouth – I know!

There is nothing whatever he can do about that.

He can smother his conscience. He can enjoy his money. But he is not, never will be, and never can be – safe.

Nevertheless, he can do a formidable amount of damage before he is caught.

How To Avoid Acts Of Treason

(In Six Not-So-Easy Lessons)

1. If you find yourself in touch with Russian or likewise officials, mention the matter to a superior officer or your industrial or departmental security officer. He will give you advice, and you may be able to continue the association if you are so advised or if you wish. Keep him informed all the time. It costs nothing, and is easy.

2. If you become friendly with a foreigner, especially officialdom from a hostile theatre, ask yourself two questions:
    a. Is he really seeking friendship – or information?
    b. Why should he choose me in order to learn, for example, about "the British way of life"?

3. Avoid performing any paid service, however innocent it may seem, for foreign officialdom. It could be the beginning of the end for you, but bear in mind common sense and diplomacy will also be in play here.

4. If you are already, innocently enough, friendly with any of these people and have not reported the matter, safeguard yourself by doing so at once. Your forgetfulness will doubtless be overlooked this time. If you are abroad, let's say in Russia or any hostile theatre, remember that you may be led into a trap or blackmailed. Do not make the mistake of thinking that you could be of no use to an enemy intelligence service. You might be.

5. If you work in an embassy or any industry in a hostile theatre, remember that you will almost certainly be assessed as a potential recruit, willing or unwilling. Try to live sensibly and soberly, and not become too isolated from the British community. But if anything goes wrong – tell the Embassy. It will not surprise them in any way. They've heard it all before.

How To Engage In Treason

(In Six Easy Lessons)

1. Let it be known to your friends, casual acquaintances, and strangers that you have access to secret information, or are in a job where you may be able to obtain it one day. Remember we spoke earlier about the attention seeker? This should attract treasonable propositions or threats, which it may or may not be possible to resist.

2. Always think you are cleverer than you are. Be conceited. Tell yourself that you are fully capable of handling any regular association with foreign officialdom on a casual basis without informing your superior officer or local security officer. If the foreign contact is a diplomat, convince yourself that it's only your fascinating personality, wit, and friendship that attracts him. If you can believe that, you can believe anything. Don't worry – you're well on your way.

3. Develop a few vices, especially abroad so that with luck you can be compromised and blackmailed.

4. If you cannot manage a vice or two, just be plain foolish. Play the stupid card for all it's worth. If you can't be foolish, be incautious.

5. Accept favours and hospitality from Russian or other hostile officials, so that you put yourself under an obligation to them. When, in return, and they will, ask for some harmless service in exchange for good money, accept at once. This encourages them, and, if you pursue the matter to a logical conclusion, make no mistake, you should land yourself safely in prison one day.

6. If, by chance, you do not fancy prison, especially in cold weather, persuade yourself that if you become a spy, you will never get caught. You will, of course, in the end, but one must not start this treacherous fallacy with a defeatist attitude.

Security Defences

Since we now live in a much more modern and increasingly dangerous world the threat of espionage is very grave and on the increase and quite a lot is known about the way spies are recruited and operationally controlled, it is common sense to take steps to make spying more difficult and more dangerous. This is what modern security is about and its objectives are:

- A. To prevent anyone having access to secrets who is not authorised to see them;
- B. To ensure that everyone who is authorised to have access to secrets is trustworthy, disciplined, and alert;

and,

- C. By the application of the "need to know" principle and in other ways to minimise the damage a spy can do if he gets inside the defences, to maximise the risks he has to run and to facilitate his detection when suspicion has been aroused.

Physical (which includes document) security may sound dull, but it is a matter of vital importance. The following passages give some advice on how you can achieve it. Even for our present day professionals but certainly for our future training theatres they are very worth reading if only to refresh the mind.

Physical security, tiresome at first, can become a habit which, once acquired, becomes as much a part of daily routine as cleaning the teeth.

How To Foil A Spy

(Some Advice On)

1. Read and observe your departmental security instructions conscientiously. They have been drafted by people who understand the threat of espionage and are designed to help fight it and its consequences.

2. Don't discuss classified information outside the office or as a member of the Armed Forces. Inside the office or military unit always follow the "need to know" principle. This is the rule that a particular piece of information is not passed on to a person who does not require it – even though such a person is authorised to handle other secret information. This principle being if a person simply doesn't know something there is no way, even under legal or illegal pressure, or torture, that he can give it away.

   Apart from anything else, there is the chance that, since he does not deal with the subject himself, he may not appreciate its significance to a spy, or safeguard it with the same care as you do.

   It should indeed be a matter of etiquette and good manners not to seek information to which you are not entitled. It places a colleague in the embarrassing position of either having to refuse you, or else break the rule. And this rule stands despite all the casual flippancy we see going on between "Bond" and "Moneypenny" in that insecure outer office as he throws his hat across the room! That is "spook" fiction. Discarding the "need to know" principle in our modern spy wars can lead to death and destruction.

3. Keep the office tidy. Official material may otherwise get hidden by other things.

4. Keep classified papers in your desk or table or in the appropriate container. Don't take classified papers to the canteens, washrooms, or cloakrooms.
5. Observe the rules about locking up at lunchtime and during short absences from the room.
6. Check all classified material is put away securely at the end of each day. Do not overlook the security of computers, especially laptops.
7. Don't leave security keys where unauthorised people can get at them, even for a few seconds – a wax impression can be taken in a matter of moments.
8. Don't keep classified papers loose. Attach them as soon as you can to a file. Loose papers are sparkling champagne to a spy, but papers that have been properly filed cannot be removed without leaving a gap in the file that may be noticed.
9. Avoid over-classifying papers. When you have classified a document, ask yourself: "Could I safely and sensibly give this a lower classification?" Too many papers to guard means that the important ones receive less attention than they should.
10. Don't take classified material away from the office, even when you are travelling officially, unless it is strictly necessary to the purpose of your business, and you know you have fully complied with the rules.
11. Don't even discuss secrets or classified matters on the open telephone.
12. Do not use a telephone number, the date of a birthday, or any other obvious number, for the setting of any combination locks or this twenty-first century's array of implements we have to contend with and never write the combination of digits in a diary – or in any other insecure place, even in code.
13. Take care of your ID card, pass, or any similar document. They are very attractive gate-keys!
14. See that the windows and doors of the building are secure at the end of the day, if such is your responsibility. Burglaries by spies may not have been very frequent of old but there is now, and

will be serious opportunity in our new "Cold War". For reasons beyond most of us there are many scantily vetted peripherals wandering our corridors under the guise of "Human Resources". Now, whether that means cleaning-maintenance-sub-contractual elements, or that old chestnut security, to me, and to you it shouldn't really matter, these people have blank-cheque access to what should be classed as sterile areas and this is why all the above notes on security of classified material must be treated as second nature by all.

15. Throughout all of the stories in this book I hope I have put to you how easy it is in the world of espionage to wallow in, or to avoid catastrophe. You can avoid it so easily. Don't ever hesitate to ask the advice of your Commanding Officer, division, branch, section or industrial security representative. Report to him, or her, anything you think may be of security interest. It will be treated confidentially.

16. Good Hunting. But always remember, in this game the hunter never comes home from the Hill!

The work is never complete.

"Conclusive Brief"

Call it what you will – spying, treason, cover deception. It's as old as mankind yet as modern as the new age political correctness, which bedevils us in our efforts to support this slippery old fish we call democracy.

The very rule of Law continues to beat us mercilessly, and when bleeding and almost broken we seldom get more than a recovering splash of water from our persistent tormentor – the Human Rights "Card Player"!

For the Police, the Armed Forces, and the Security Services we know the dangers of imported spying from Russia, China, and the Middle East, but our operatives at the coal-face – *where the god-like never go* – would at times be forgiven for thinking another enemy, much more dangerous than most, persistently hovers.

This enemy, for the active service operative in a CQB situation (close quarter battle) – and make no mistake, it is a modern battle we fight in civilian clothes – this enemy I would describe to you as that 'millisecond' of decision as to whether or not to slip the safety and destroy the one you believe to be the intended hostile target.

When your finger milks that trigger you enter that red haze of human frailty where the world of billion-pound technology cannot save you from the fickle principles of this democracy where we work, sometimes to the point of dying to defend its policy.

For me, this brings to mind something to do with "a rock and a hard place". All those on the job will know what I mean!

As you will see, most stories we have looked at refer to the period of the first Cold War. But now, as we approach the end of the first decade of this new century it is so important to bear in mind, with an émigré system in chaos, and borders as wide open as the Grand Canyon, (the words of Government Ministers circa 2007), the opportunity here in Britain for any Hostile Intelligence Agency cannot, and must not be spin-bound or underestimated.

For the existence and success of spies in any émigré system in flux, in even the most policed democracy, the world need not be enough, as Bond would say to Moneypenny, for the world is their oyster.

Within that system which undertakes a Government backed policy of walking on egg-shells for the sake of political correctness and every unflinching aspect of the Human Rights Act and its exuberant supporters, that system had better prepare itself for covert infiltrated chaos as sleeper agents embedded, soon learn they have never had it so good. And why?

For my analysis, the main problems seem to be the general public's lack of interest and knowledge in most areas of security. A sense of, "nothing to do with me, mate!"

In my recent experience, and I'm sorry to say even within the Military Theatre, if I mention: Lonsdale, Burgess, McLean, Philby, or Blunt, not to forget Fuchs, the average person even up to the age of forty, would think I was talking of some Irish boy-band, or an unexpected shake-up at Arsenal FC.

I would consider this as worrying as it would seem to suggest we have a reincarnation of the same brand of unawareness and national attitude in general as we had when, between 1935 and 1939, people fell around laughing as Churchill tried to warn just what a monster was brewing in the bowels of industrial Germany.

In September '39 the mirth and doubting laughter soon faded!

The time has come again when the public must be educated in duty and responsibility and into understanding both industrially and militarily that age-old chestnut:

"Loose talk really does cost lives!"

As we mentioned before, the spy or terrorist depends on our persistent pacification of the Human Rights "God-like" manual by the very system he would seek to damage. So be aware, that that system had better prepare itself and its forces for covert, and at times even overt, intrusive spying. It will flourish because freedom is their great ally. They have nothing to fear but fear itself.

One of our main problems here would seem to be the public's lack of investigative interest in security matters at national level. 007 is all very well, but take away the armchair and the TV and all else is just too much trouble.

Those, I fear too many, who buy a newspaper today only do so for two genres therein. The first being the initial four pages encompassing the latest demeaning drivel against celebrity, and the overall national status in today's Britain. Then, of course, the last six pages of sports news.

Fearful intellectualism!

Completely overlooked are the periodic but importantly informative essays by people "in the know", as it were to World affairs. These writings are usually buried within the core of the paper, and unfortunately, flicked through and dismissed as if there, only, but only, for the intelligencia.

And there, as they say, lies the rub! An almost total civilian ignorance of an enemy in their midst.

When the bombs are detonated, a whole myriad of people in uniform, not to mention the Security Services are said to be negligent and at fault.

Because of their limited knowledge of terrorist tactics and habits the public and media in general fail to grasp the problems at hand and how the Security and Intelligence Services cannot hope to anticipate every last move of the hostile operative.

Let me give you a spurious situation as an explanatory example and try to understand it this way; science and technology does not play a pivotal part in "basic" terror or spying.

You can choke the Thames estuary with aircraft carriers, block the channel with submarines and blacken the skies with technical wizardry, but all that combined power cannot, and will not stop that one "lilywhite". That is to say, that one unknown new recruit, as he toddles across Waterloo Bridge at 08.00 on Monday morning amongst thousands of other unknowns.

Along he goes in his flat cap and donkey jacket with his "ample lunch box" under his arm and his rolled up newspaper sticking out from his pocket as he trailbreaks his casual way to the main concourse at the packed railway station.

His "lunchbox" can kill 100 on site, fill the hospitals, and send shock waves around the civilised world.

With no hum'int – (human intelligence) on that one insidious grubby little man, nothing on this earth could have stopped him from delivering his message. And yet, no one stops to think of the intricacies of this before they jump and scream "foul" in the direction of the Security Intelligence Services.

Perhaps it's not the fault of the public or media while they suffer a complete lack of understanding.

Maybe they should read Eye Spy magazine or perhaps this small publication to give them some understanding of the dangerous years ahead. I would hope it might help all, from primary school pupil before they reach those older, but influential years and right up to any sceptics we may have, even at Government level.

As this book goes to press, within the Military there are a number of security "situations" in progress. I have mentioned one very briefly in the foreword. It was reference a Corporal accused of helping Iran with information during the 2006 war footing with Afghanistan. On that we can only wait and see what damage was done.

In this book, with the kind permission of the COI – Central Office of Information – Crown Copyright, I would like to think, for the purposes of information and education, I have brought some things to light which would benefit the Armed Forces at levels of contact from the Foot-Soldier through to the Officer Core. As we have read, the areas of vulnerability are widespread.

I must add here, of my twenty-two years service in both Army and Royal Marines, I have never read of the security dangers, in depth, in any ship or unit standing orders. This is why I believe a better understanding is needed for Company, Battalion, and Commando RM level. The RAF, RN and many other peripheral elements should not be ignored. It is within the "need to know" guideline.

The Director General of MI5 warned in an address to the Society of Editors in Manchester in October 2007 titled Intelligence, Counter Intelligence and Trust, that people as young as 15 were being groomed and recruited for illegal hostile activities.

"As I speak, Terrorists are methodically and intentionally targeting young people and children in this country. They are radicalising, indoctrinating and grooming young, vulnerable people to carry out acts of terrorism. This year we have seen individuals as young as 15–16 implicated in terrorist-related activity."

"There have been high levels of covert activity by foreign intelligence organisations in our country. Since the end of the last cold war we have seen no decrease in the numbers of undeclared Russian intelligence officers in the UK – at the Russian Embassy and associated organisations conducting covert activity within the UK."

The dangers are here now, just as always, and on the increase for national and personal security. They may have scorned Churchill and lived to regret it, but we must not now laugh at the persistent warnings we receive from the Intelligence Services.

As we now enter our second and in my view even bigger cold war it is essential that people are much more aware of what's actually going on all around them.

To finish and perhaps make a final point, if you should seek my opinion on the security situation in Britain and her overseas interests between now, circa 2008 and 2025, I would simply ask you to recall this order given by Captain Bligh aboard HMS *Bounty*, which should give it to you fairly and squarely…

"Prepare the ship for heavy weather Mr Christian."

The State of Play

On the cover of this book you will read the words Vigilance-Duty-Responsibility. But it is irresponsibility that promotes those feel good, politically correct teachings which are creating a generation, (or two), of youth with no concept of reality, and how it sets them up for failure in the real world.

I believe it was with this in mind the Director General of MI5 warned of the grooming of youth, home grown and émigré, in the direction of terrorist activity. It starts with peripheral gentility, but once the seeds are planted, at least a partial blossoming to full-blown terrorist acts are inevitable.

On the streets of our cities and towns, when the sun goes down each night, the display of angst, anger and the demand for *'respect'* is rolled out by the deluded, for all to see. It is within this playground that golden opportunities flourish for the talent spotters of hostile Intelligence Agencies of terror, with their endless supply of *smart* promises and enticements, especially within ethnic groupings.

'And the hungry youth feed'!

A meaningful section of these lost souls inevitably fall foul to radicalising indoctrinating and professional grooming. They delusively believe this is where they will find that much sought after *'respect'*.

Remember what we said about conceit and vanity:

> A sense of power - of being part of a strong machine.
> A love of intrigue.
> Feelings of importance.
> A desire for praise and flattery.

The answer?

Responsible adult integration, association, and open trust and challenge. Most young people are hugely responsive to a cold, hard reality check.

The honest laying down of the laws of life were at play recently in the USA when an American multi-billionaire gave a speech to a mid-west High School. I cannot quote in detail everything he said, but in essence it was what I would now say to multi-cultural British youth, on their immediate future.

The real facts of 'respect'!

Rule 1: Life is not fair - get used to it.

Rule 2: The world won't care about your self-esteem. You will be expected to accomplish something *before* you should feel good about yourself.

Rule 3: You will not make £50,000 a year straight out of school. You won't be Chairman or M.D with a car phone until you earn both.

Rule 4: If you think the local police and your teachers are tough, wait until you get a real boss.

Rule 5: Washing tables is not beneath your dignity and your grandparents had a different word for sweeping factory floors - they called it *opportunity.*

Rule 6: If you fail on something through negligence, it's not your parents' fault, so don't whine about your mistakes, learn from them.

Rule 7: Before you were born, your parents weren't as boring as you choose to see them now. They became that way from paying your bills, cleaning your clothes, and listening to how cool you think you are.

Rule 8: Your school may have done away with winners and losers, but real life *has not.* In some schools they have abolished failing grades and they'll give you as many times as you want to get the right answer. This doesn't bear the slightest resemblance, even in your wildest dreams, to *anything* in real life.

Rule 9: Life is not divided into holidays. You don't get long hot summers off and very few employers are interested in offering you a *'gap year'* to *'find yourself'*. Do that on your own time.

Rule 10: Vacuous celebrity and television is *not* real life. In real life people have to kick off the slippers, leave the couch behind to go out and do jobs.

Rule 11: Be nice to overpowering fools, chances are you'll end up working for one.

Rule 12: The same as rule 1. Forget it at your peril.

And a final exit thought to all:

If you can read this book... thank a teacher.

If you can read it in English... thank a soldier.

Amen to that.

David Griffin
RMA. RNA
Ringwood, Hampshire
May 2008

Notes

Notes

Notes

Notes

Notes

Notes

Notes

Telephone

Telephone